WORD
WATCHER'S
HANDBOOK

Also by Phyllis Martin

Martin's Magic Formula for Getting the Right Job

"If I went back to college again, I'd concentrate on two areas: learning to write, and to speak before an audience. Nothing in life is more important than the ability to communicate effectively."

—Gerald R. Ford

WORD WATCHER'S HANDBOOK

A Deletionary of the Most Abused and Misused Words

Phyllis Martin, friends, and many readers of the first two editions

ST. MARTIN'S PRESS
New York

Production Editor: David Stanford Burr

Library of Congress Cataloging-in-Publication Data

Martin, Phyllis Rodgers.
     Word watcher's handbook : a deletionary of the most abused and misused words / Phyllis Martin.—3rd ed.
         p.   cm.
     Includes index.
     ISBN 0-312-05540-4
     ISBN 0-312-05541-2 (pbk.)
     1. English language—Usage. 2. English language—Errors of usage.
I. Title.
PE1460.M29   1991
428.1—dc20   90-19112
                                      CIP

THIRD EDITION: February 1991

The material for "Reviewing Foreign Menu Terms" is reprinted with permission from *Executive Etiquette*, copyright © 1979 by Marjabelle Young Stewart and Marian G. Faux. St. Martin's Press, New York.

The French pronunciation key is reprinted with permission from the *Larousse English/French: French/English Modern Dictionary,* copyright © Librairie Larousse, 1960, Librairie Larousse, Paris.

The spelling test beginning on page 125 is reprinted with permission from Reporter Typographics, Inc., 254 Warner Street, Cincinnati, Ohio 45219 [(513) 421-1162].

ACKNOWLEDGMENTS

First, to Ann Landers. Her mastery of the well-cast sentence is legendary; to have her say *she* learned from *Word Watcher's Handbook* is the most cherished and enduring encouragement I've experienced. That encouragement has motivated me to stay with the screamingly hard task of revising this edition.

To William Safire for citing me in his "On Language" column on two glorious occasions and then for allowing me to use *his words* in *my* book.

To Bob Braun for his enthusiasm for my deletionary. Bob's awesome gift for selling to his viewers a product in which he believes helped to force numerous printings and a second and third edition.

Thanks also to my husband, Bruce, and my daughter, Shirlie Briggs, for editorial help; to son Kipp, for his clipping service; to son Jay, for his list; to my sister, Carolyn Carter; and to all those cousins who are a part of the "Cousins' Crusade."

And to Jeffrey G. Allen, Barbara Anderson, Marja Barrett, Cynthia Browne, Ruth Cavin, Hope Dellon, Harry Engstom, Gloria Exler, Major Thomas E. Gardner, Marion Glaser, Peter P. Graham, Lou Hampton, Emilie Jacobson, Merlin James, Debbie Johnson, Jared Kieling, Andrea Krys, Herbert M. Martin, Dr. William McGrane, John E.

Moore, Mary Pascal, Priscilla Petty, Larry Pigg, Sally Richardson, Joyce Rosencrans, Dr. Morleen Rouse, Ann Marie Sabath, Ruth Schay, Joseph Speier, Vada Stanley, Bob and Evelyn Steinman, Ruth Van Gelder Bochner, and Dr. Ann Stace Wood.

CONTENTS

FOREWORD ix
INTRODUCTION 1
    Listening 5
    Sample Flash Cards 6
1. DELETIONARY 11
    Runners-up 20
    Feeble-phrase Finder 21
2. USAGE 36
    Unmatched Pairs 53
3. PRONUNCIATION PITFALLS 62
4. BEYOND THE BASICS 79
    Out-of-it Words/On-top-of-it Words 80
    Brand Names 84
    An Awareness Test 86
5. REVIEWING FOREIGN MENU TERMS 91
    French Cuisine 92
    Italian Cuisine 101
6. ENGLISH AS A SECOND LANGUAGE FOR
    AMERICANS 105
    American English/English English 106
    American Spelling/English Spelling 110
    British Place Names 110

7. TRAVELER'S ADVISORY: WELCOME
   WORDS   112
   A Quick Quiz to Test Your Travel Savvy   112
8. OCCUPATIONAL HAZARDS OF THE
   VERBAL VARIETY   119
9. CLEARING A PATH IN THE WORDS   127
   Word Exorcises   127
10. COMING TO TERMS: A WORD WATCHER'S
    GLOSSARY   149
    General Business Terms   149
    Computer Terms   154
    Satellite Terms   156

BIBLIOGRAPHY   157

Now a Word from You, Please   159

Order Form   160

Index   161

FOREWORD

This book is about words. In particular, it is about words that are harmful to a vibrant, healthy vocabulary. It's a *deletionary,* a handy compendium of misused words and clichés that ought to be drummed out of our vocabularies for good. Culling such deadwood will not diminish our ability to communicate; it will produce a leaner, clearer, more effective way to do so. My guess is that we remember that memo from Moses as much for crispness as for content. There's nothing ambiguous or fuzzy about "Thou shalt not kill, thou shalt not steal."

All our lives we've been urged to add words to our vocabularies. Isn't it time we were encouraged to delete feeble phrases and abused or misused words from our speech and writing?

The first edition of *Word Watcher's Handbook* evolved from a "word clinic" I give for almost any business, professional, educational, or social group that asks me. The second edition was born because so many readers responded to the first edition and asked me to include their "wince words" next time around. This—the third edition—is necessary due to additional reader response and because this fluid language of ours makes an update necessary.

My goal is lofty:

To save the job seeker from a possible turndown.
To improve the job holder's chances for promotion.
To inspire the student to master the most important tool
  he or she will ever use: language.
To help everyone avoid embarrassing mistakes in every-
  day conversation.

My ultimate aim is to help every reader delete conversational cholesterol that clogs lines of communication.

A college graduate should manage to lose a minimum of five words. A high school graduate should manage to lose ten to twenty unwanted words. Younger students and dropouts can lose up to fifty in the first week.

You astute readers will notice that certain words have been cited several times. This repetition is deliberate for it serves as reinforcement.

INTRODUCTION

Words are tools of the brain. We blunt them at our peril. Consider this example: A candidate for a post on the President's Council on Aging was rejected because she pronounced Illinois "Ill•ih•noise." She was to have represented the Chicago area. After hearing her speak, the hiring committee was no longer interested in her.

In his performance-appraisal interview, Wallace B. said to his manager, "Let me *ax* you just one question."

The manager winced when he heard the word **ask** pronounced *ax*. It was all he could do to refrain from clenching his fist as he pretended not to have heard. In order to be fair, he asked Wallace to repeat what he'd just said. Indeed, it was *ax*.

Up to that point Wallace had been under consideration for an important promotion. The interview continued for some time, but it was actually over the moment the one word *ax* was used.

Dave shouted, "*Irregardless* of what you say, I'm going to get a *pitcher* of you."

Dave's camera clicked, but he didn't. For Sue ran across the lawn in the opposite direction. When a friend asked if Dave's approach had been too strong, Sue said yes and his language too weak.

• • •

How many times have you heard errors like these, as jarring to the ear as static on a radio? You are more aware of the error than of the content of what has just been said. Worst of all, the speaker has no idea that he or she has made a mistake.

Or perhaps you have heard a word pronounced differently from the way you always thought it was pronounced, and thought, I wonder if I've been saying that right? You intend to look it up but somehow never do.

Even if you are a fairly well-read person with a reasonably good vocabulary, there may be just a few errors you are making that are as painful to some people as the errors above are to you. As you begin to read through this book, you are likely to be surprised at the number of errors that have slipped into your everyday speech.

The first three chapters of *Word Watcher's Handbook* are designed to attack a specific category of language misuse. The first chapter, "Deletionary," lists words you should remove from your vocabulary, either because they are hackneyed and trite (and may leave a similar impression of you) or because they simply are not words. The worst offenders are harmful to the health of your vocabulary. They're poison—throw them away forever. The second part of the deletionary is a list of feeble phrases that may have been original at one time but have long since lost their punch.

Chapter 2, "Usage," contains words that are frequently misused. Included in this chapter is the section Unmatched Pairs, which lists pairs of words that sound alike or are frequently confused, with short explanations of which one to use when.

Chapter 3, "Pronunciation Pitfalls," is a selection of commonly mispronounced words and an easy-to-read guide to the correct way to say them.

Here is the foolproof method for making sure the boners in this book will never appear in your speech:

As you go through the book, make a flash card for each word you were wrong about or unsure of, following the illustrations on pages 7–9. It may seem like busywork, as you measure and snip the cards and carefully print the words, but do it. You will be rewarded later by the convenience. You will also be more likely to discipline yourself to study words that trouble you—once through the flash cards each day and you're finished. Put those cards out in plain view on your nightstand or desk, where they will remind you of their existence. Remember, the task will get shorter each day as you throw away the cards you no longer need.

If you become bored with the flash card method and like to fool around with tape recorders, try this method for variety: Make a recording of the words you would like to learn, leaving a gap of about five seconds after each word. If it is meaning you are trying to remember, pronounce the word correctly on the tape and give yourself enough time to write down the meaning on a blank sheet of paper before going on. Then compare your paper with this book and grade yourself. If you are working on pronunciation, say into the microphone, "How do you pronounce C-H-A-S-M?" You can write down the correct pronunciations.

You can also simply make a tape of the words that you have trouble pronouncing. Just hearing them over and over again as you get dressed or drive your car can help to impress them in your memory. It's best not to record any wrong pronunciations, even for test purposes, because hearing the word mispronounced will hamper your ear training.

Now for a few final touches that will improve your communication with others. Even perfect speech will not be effective unless you keep the listener in mind in the following ways:

• Beware of the sheer length of some words. They are tiring to a listener's ears. If it's clarity of communication that you seek, try plain, sturdy, surefooted words; then, if you can't resist a long word, your listener will have the strength to absorb it.

- Don't make bounding leaps in your speech, leaving out the essential intermediate steps—or, even worse, filling in with "you knows," "uhms," and "et ceteras." Be articulate; the listener needs to be carefully led. If you can't express what you mean clearly, imagine how fuzzy the listener's picture will be.
- To keep an audience's attention, make sure your speech is full of visual images. Examples are an excellent means of creating pictures.
- Learn to improve the pitch and volume of your own voice. Listen to yourself on a tape recorder, at least, and take a few voice-training lessons if you think you need them. You can be taught to lower the pitch of your voice, for instance.
- Use your dictionary as those hardworking lexicographers intended. Know that the job of the lexicographer is to *report* usage, not to arbitrate it. The fact that you see a word in a dictionary does not mean the writers of the dictionary sanction the word in question. That is why many dictionaries contain special "correct usage" or "common error" sections.
- Read, but be careful about trying out new words before you are sure of their pronunciation.
- Go to a lecture now and then instead of a movie.
- Listen to a talk show on the radio, or watch one on television, instead of a situation comedy.
- Remember your normal share of speaking time is only 50 percent in a conversation with one other person. It is proportionately less with a larger group. Exceed that share only when you are sure others agree you should.
- Finally, don't allow all these dos and don'ts to ruin brisk, original, pleasant speech. Be spontaneous and say things your way.

LISTENING

A large part of communicating well is listening well. Listen closely to the others instead of concentrating on what you're going to say next; then what you do say will make more sense. The most polished speech will sound foolish if you are not following the thread of the conversation.

Even more important, when you take the time to hear and understand what the other person is really saying, you save marriages, friendships, and jobs and you learn the true art of communication.

Answer the following questions about yourself, and look back at them after a few weeks to see if you are improving your listening skills.

Are you a positive listener?

Do you say to the speaker, "Tell me about it"?

Do you give encouragement to the speaker and reassurance from time to time that you are with him or her?

Do you look at the speaker?

Do you follow the speaker's ideas a little further, asking specific questions and trying to hit on what the speaker's deepest interest in the subject is?

Do you listen for clues to what the speaker's interests are and search for an area of mutual interest?

Do you echo important messages, to make sure you understood them?

Are you a negative listener?

Do you say to the speaker, "I know just what you're going to say"?

Do you say, "We've tried that before" as soon as the speaker begins an explanation, or, just as bad, when he or she is finished?

Do you look away from the speaker?

Do you think you know someone else's point of view before he or she tells you?

Do you decide in advance that you know more about the subject than the speaker does?

Do you decide ahead of time that the subject is dull? That the speaker is dull?

Do you find the merest pretext to turn the conversation back to yourself, your preoccupations, or your ideas?

A special note about the written word: The late Commerce Secretary Malcolm Baldrige had a dandy idea for eliminating irritating words from letters, speeches, and manuscripts.

The electronic word processors in his office were set up so that if an employee punched in one of forty-three forbidden words or phrases, a warning was flashed.

DON'T USE THAT WORD.

Many of the words on the secretary's list are in this book because they annoy other people, too. Some of the forbidden terms are **viable, interface, prioritize,** and **needless to say.**

So, why not make a list of terms your boss, your editor, or your friends don't like or that you misuse, and feed them into your word processor?

Finally, a word of advice that has nothing to do with speaking, or listening: Kind words are more important than the kinds of words you use.

SAMPLE FLASH CARDS

You can use different colors of paper for deletions, definitions, and pronunciations.

Deletionary

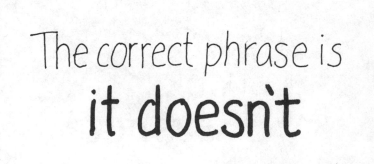

I must delete the phrase
it don't
from my vocabulary

Front

The correct phrase is
it doesn't

Back

Usage

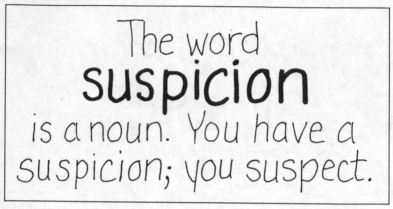

The word
suspicion
is a noun. You have a
suspicion; you suspect.

Front

Do not say,
I suspicion;
say I **suspect.**

Back

Pronunciation

The correct pronunciation of **realtor** is **ree´·ul·tr**

Front

Re al tor
that's **al** in the middle of the word, not **la**

Back

1

DELETIONARY

When you use too many words, you tire your listener and make it more difficult for him to hear the important words. You can also give the impression that you are fond of the sound of your own voice, when in truth you are just speaking as you are used to speaking, with all the bad habits you have picked up along the way. This chapter will guide you in clearing away the excess words and phrases that are cluttering your speech. It will help to make you into one of those admirable people of whom it is said, "He spoke a few well-chosen words."

Some of the words in this deletionary are just plain wrong and make a far worse impression of you than verbosity does. If the nonwords that follow have crept into your speech, make that flash card now, and be sure that when the card is finally thrown away, the nonword is gone forever, too.

The list includes trite and overused expressions as well as wordy and wrong ones. Notice that although old clichés are dreary, there is nothing more warmed-over sounding than yesterday's slang.

absolutely	Don't use this word when you mean **yes**.
accidently	You mean **accidentally**. Pronounce all five syllables: **ak•si•den•tahl•lee**.

acrost, acrossed	The word you want is **across.**
advance planning	What other kind of planning is there? The same goes for *advance warning.*
afeared	This is a corruption of the word **afraid.** Please delete it from your vocabulary.
ahold	Not standard English. Drop the **a.**
ain't	Colloquial. **Is not** and **are not** are preferable.
all things being equal	What could this possibly mean, when you think about it?
alot	Do not make one word from two. Say **a lot.**
and stuff	A filler phrase, to make your statement sound more complete than it is.
and that	Same as *and stuff.*
anyways	Say **anyway.**
anywheres	No **s** here either; it's **anywhere.**
aren't I	When you use this phrase, you are contracting the words *are I not.* **Am I not** is preferred to *aren't I.*
ascared	Not standard English. The words are **scared** and **afraid.**
as you know	If they know, you shouldn't be telling them again. **As you may know** makes more sense, but don't use it just to be polite.
at this point in time	One of the many verbose phrases that should be replaced by good old **now.**
balance	Don't use this word as a substitute for **rest,** although you may use it when speaking of money: **The balance is due when we pick up the chair.**
basket case	Not a nice expression, especially if it's used for what it means.
beautiful!	Appropriate about once a year.
beautiful person	Doesn't this phrase imply that everyone else isn't beautiful? *Beautiful person* is passé now, and it's about time. The sim-

ple **I like him** has more force than *He's a beautiful person.*

be that as it may	Archaic and pedantic-sounding. The word **but** will do.
blame it on	You can **blame** a person, or **put the blame on** him.
boughten	A nonword. Use **bought.**
bretzel	You mean **pretzel;** and it starts with **p.**
bust	Avoid saying *bust* when you mean **burst.**
can	Don't use as a substitute for **may.** *Can* denotes ability; **may** denotes permission.
can't hardly	This is a double negative and should not be used. Say **can hardly.**
case	Don't use as a substitute for **instance** or **example.** *In most cases* should be **In most instances.**
character	Slang when used to mean a "unique personality."
charisma	Once a lovely word meaning "a special gift of the Holy Spirit," *charisma* is now applied to everyone from politicians to underground movie stars.
chauvinist	How about saying, for example, **He's condescending to women?** It's more specific, less rhetorical.
clean, clear	These words should not be used to describe degree. *Clean up to here* and *clear up to here* should be eliminated.
cold slaw	It is **cole slaw.**
complected	The word is **complexioned.**
confrontation	Sometimes **meeting** will do.
consciousness raising	Overused. How about **deepening awareness** for the sake of variety?
consensus of opinion	The idea of *opinion* is built into the word **consensus.**
continue on	Redundant. Just say **continue.**

cool	An overworked fad word from the fifties.
curiously enough	Say **curiously**. It's more effective.
disadvantaged	A euphemism for **poor**.
drapes	It's **draperies**.
drownded	The past tense of **drown** is **drowned**.
due to the fact that	Just say **because**. By the way, only a thing can be *due* to another thing. You cannot say, for instance, *We capsized, due to the heavy wind;* you must say **because of**.
emote	Not a word. To **show emotion** is the equivalent, or you may be more precise.
encounter	**Meet?**
enthused	Not a word. Say **enthusiastic**.
equally as	Redundant. Just say **equally**.
escalate	There's nothing wrong with this new word, except that it's overused.
estimated at about	Delete the *about:* That's part of the meaning of **estimate**.
et	Not a word. Say **we have eaten** or **we ate**—never *we et.*
evacuate	To make empty. For example, **The building was evacuated** (not *The tenants were evacuated*).
excape	The word you want is **escape**. There is no **x** in the word.
expertise	Use **knowledge** or **experience** for a change.
famed	A self-conscious coinage by the mass media, as if to say, "He's famed, and *we* famed him." **Famous** is still preferred.
fantastic	Overworked. Try **fanciful, odd, grotesque.** When it is used to express vague positive feelings, it is sadly misused.
finalize	**Finish, complete, conclude?**

flustrated	A combination of **flustered** and **frustrated**? Be precise, and use one or the other.
for free	**Free** or **for nothing** are fine, but *for free* sounds childish.
frame of reference	**Background? Viewpoint? Academic discipline?**
gent	Say **gentleman** or **man.**
gross	Overused. Try **vulgar** or **coarse.**
growth	To those who laud all *growth,* I say, "Remember cancer and kudzu." Use **increase in size** or **volume.**
guesstimate	Do you mean "a very rough estimate"? Say so. *Guesstimate* may have been mildly amusing the first time it was used.
heartrendering	If you must use this tired expression, make it **heartrending.** You render fat, not hearts.
heighth	Not a word. The term you want is **height.** Pronounce it **hite** (rhymes with **kite**).
herewith	Herewith means "enclosed with this," so it is redundant to say *enclosed herewith.* Just say **Herewith is the package I promised you.**
hinderance	Though derived from the word **hinder,** this verb's noun form is **hindrance,** and it has only two syllables.
hisself	Not a word. The correct word is **himself.**
hopefully	Say **I hope** or even plain old **perhaps:** The hope is sometimes evident in the context.
how about that?	A tired old nonremark.
hunnert	The word you want is **hundred.**
I been	Say **I have been.**

I done	**I have done,** or **I did.**
I don't think	How can you express an opinion if you don't think? Try **I think not.** The phrase *I don't think* hurts many ears.
incidently	The word is **incidentally,** and it has five syllables.
in my opinion, I think	**I think** is sufficient. *In my personal opinion* is of the same order.
insightful	Overused. Try **discerning, intuitive, penetrating.**
irregardless	The word is **regardless.**
it don't	This is a contraction of *it do not,* an incorrect phrase. Say **it does not** or **it dosen't.**
learning experience	One either learns from experience or one doesn't; the phrase is meaningless.
love	If **like** will do, you're using the word **love** too loosely.
marginal	When used in phrases such as *a marginal difference,* the word means nothing that **small** doesn't mean. Unless you're referring to a margin, say **small.**
meaningful dialogue meaningful experience meaningful relationship	The word *meaningful* evokes a negative response in many people. I've had complaints about *meaningful* dialogue, *meaningful* experience, and *meaningful* relationship.
muchly	Avoid. This word was all right in Shakespeare's time, but it is considered affected and incorrect today.
my personal opinion	If it's your opinion, then by definition it's personal.
needless to say	A filler. If it were needless, you wouldn't be saying it.
never before in the past	Pick one: **before** or **in the past.**
nowheres	The word is **nowhere** (without the **s**).
off of	Omit the *of.* **Get off the bus.**

okay? When used intermittently in a narrative, this word annoys the listener by begging for his approval.

ongoing Most sentences featuring *ongoing* are strengthened by omitting it.

orientate Not standard English. Say **orient.**

oughta Not standard English. Say **ought to** or **should.**

out loud **Aloud** is preferred.

out of Use with care. In some phrases the *of* is superfluous, as in *look out of the window or walk out of the door.* Unless you're a termite, make that **out the door.** You can only get out of something you have been in; i.e., you can **walk out of a building.**

overly The prefix **over-** sounds better, or just say **too.**

over with Omit the *with.*

personal friend In most instances, **friend** is enough.

personally, I think Same as *my personal opinion*—the *personally* is unnecessary.

plastic Let's return this one to its dictionary meaning, and to all "plastic" parents: May your offspring think of something more original.

please? If you're speaking German, you're allowed to say *Bitte?* ("Please?") meaning "What did you say?" Since many people do not understand this colloquialism, in English it is better to avoid it. Then, too, there are many who understand it but can't stand it.

presently If you mean "now," say **now.** You may use **presently** to mean "soon," but **soon** is shorter and less pretentious.

prior to Say **before.**

quote Correct as a verb (**He quoted Emerson.**

May I quote you?) but not as a noun (say **a quotation from Emerson**).

rap   For "talk," a little shopworn. **Rap music** is another matter.

really   If you're using it for emphasis, rather than to mean "as opposed to appearances," eliminate it.

relatively   *Relatively* can be nothing but an attempt to get yourself off the hook when you think you've said something too definite. If you can't say what's relative to what, chances are nothing is, and you should leave this word out. *Relatively speaking* almost always means nothing.

relevant   The word *relevant* appears in this section because so many people complained that they are tired of hearing it. You may want to say **pertinent** or **to the point.**

reoccur   The correct word is **recur.**

rewarding   Try to name what the rewards are.

right on!   Originally a political rallying cry, and now misused to express approval of what has just been said. This phrase is tired anyway and would best be marched right on out.

Sahara desert   Sahara means "desert," so just say the **Sahara.** The same goes for *Rio Grande River* and *Mount Fujiyama* (it's the **Rio Grande** and **Fujiyama,** or **Mount Fuji**).

see what I mean?   Another phrase—like *okay?*—that begs approval. Eliminate it from your vocabulary.

snuck   Not standard English. Say **sneaked.**

spastic   A word that is offensive except when correctly used as a medical term.

start off   Just say **start.** You don't need *off* after it.

supposing	The word is **suppose,** as in, **Suppose you go first.**
swang	Dialectical past tense form of **swing. Swung** is preferred.
tell it like it is	Old as old slang.
thanking you, I remain	Old and trite.
the fact is, is that	This phrase is wholly unnecessary, but the double *is* sounds tongue-tied besides.
theirselves	The word is **themselves.**
this here	If the object or person referred to is present, **this** alone is enough. If it's not present, substitute **a** for *this.* Say **A boy I met at the beach,** not *This boy I met at the beach.*
thusly	Say simply **thus.**
umble	The word is **humble.** Sound the **h.**
unbeknownst	Pompous substitute for **unknown.**
underprivileged	Say **poor** instead.
undoubtably	The word is **undoubtedly,** pronounced **un•dow′•ted•lee.**
valid	A tired word. Try **cogent. Well-grounded. Solid. Genuine.**
viable	**Possible, capable of living, alive?**
whole nother thing	The word **another** is divided and **whole** is stuck inside. Say instead, **That's another matter entirely.**
widow woman	**Widow** is sufficient. The word already encompasses the idea of woman, just as **widower** includes the idea of man.
-wise	As a handy suffix, meaning "in any way whatsoever related to the root word," **-wise** is misused.
you can say that again	Conversational overkill. You can nod politely to show that you agree.
you know	A hedge for when the speaker doesn't know how to explain something. *You*

> *know* can get to be an annoying habit; better to eliminate it altogether.

youse Please rid your vocabulary of this non-word. The plural of **you** is **you**.

RUNNERS-UP

Before we leave this section of the chapter, let me mention that almost everyone dislikes professional jargon, trendy words, and buzzwords. Teachers complain about social workers, doctors about lawyers—you get the idea: Nobody wants to be on the outside of a discussion.

Take a look at this list of runners-up in the Most Over-used Words contest. You don't have to delete these words from your vocabulary entirely, but check to see that you are not giving some of them more than their fair share of the airwaves.

alienated	obscene
articulate (as a verb)	operative
awesome	oppressed
bizarre	overreact
climate (other than the weather variety)	paranoid
	politicized
concept	posture (for "attitude")
controversial	priorize, also prioritize
credibility	rationalize
depersonalization	rhetoric
dialogue	rip-off
dynamics	scenario
elegant	share
enrichment	structure (as a verb)
exciting	substantive
expertise	superlative
holistic	thrust
impact (as a verb)	traumatic
interface	ventilate (feelings)
involved	veritable
manic	

FEEBLE-PHRASE FINDER

Many of the following phrases once evoked vivid images: some were downright poetic. But now they slip out automatically—"as a bee" following "busy" before we can stop ourselves. They evoke nothing in the listener except weariness.

You have a right to know how I compiled this list. And if you're thinking, "My, doesn't she have her nerve?" I'll agree with you. It takes nerve. Especially since a few of my favorite expressions are included.

I believe I started this back in freshman English at the University of Cincinnati. And I know I used such a list for a secretarial program I led at the executive offices of Procter & Gamble. I know, too, that all of us in personnel agreed to help each other "banish the bromide."

Naturally, an updated version of that list became part of my current Word Watchers' Clinic. But the collection you see here has many contributors: readers of the first two editions of *Word Watcher's Handbook,* my family, friends, teachers, business associates, and every person who has been part of the word clinic.

I don't stand at the podium spieling off what I think are hackneyed phrases. Participants tell me—on cards provided or by taking the floor and telling the class and me. They also tell me by phone. Or mail. And by sending word with those who sign for later sessions.

Only after many people have commented negatively on a trite expression does it make the list. Each phrase you see had numerous nay votes.

Have a nice day wasn't even included in the first edition, but it ran a close second to *You know* this time. Together they garnered more votes than all the other phrases combined. That's why they appear in this paragraph all by themselves.

These canned similes, platitudes, bromides, clichés, and old saws are long overdue for oblivion. Won't you give them the rest they deserve?

abreast of the times
absence makes the heart grow
    fonder
accidents will happen
according to one's lights
ace in the hole
acid test
add insult to injury
after all is said and done
age before beauty
a good time was had by all

all in all
all that glitters is not gold
all too soon
all to the good
all walks of life
all wool and a yard wide
all work and no play
almighty dollar
along the line
also-ran
any and all

"Today I had twenty-three 'Is it hot enough for yous,' sixteen 'Have a
nice days,' four 'Don't call me—I'll call yous,' two 'How's the world
treatin' yous,' and one 'Buzz off, Mac!'"

Reprinted by permission of the Chicago *Tribune*-New York *News* Syndicate, Inc.

a pound of flesh
apple-pie order
arms of Morpheus
as a whole
as for me
asleep at the switch
as luck would have it
as the crow flies
at death's door
at first blush
at loose ends
at the crossroads
at this point in time
at wit's end
auspicious occasion
avoided like the plague
back to the drawing board
back to the wall
banker's hours
bark up the wrong tree
bated breath
bathed in tears
bat out of hell
battle for life/of life
beard the lion in his den
beat a dead horse
beat a hasty retreat
bee in her bonnet
beg to advise
believe you me
best bib and tucker
best-laid plans of mice and
   men
better late than never
better to have loved and lost
between a rock and a hard
   place
between the devil and the deep
   blue sea
between two stools

between you, me and the
   lamppost (fence post)
bird in the hand
bite off more than one can
   chew
bite the bullet
bite the dust
bitter end
black as coal
blanket of snow
blazing inferno
blood is thicker than water
blow hot and cold
blow off steam
blow your own horn
blow your top
blushing bride
bolt from the blue
bone of contention
bone to pick
born with a silver spoon
bosom of the family
bottom line
bottom of the barrel
brain trust
break the ice
break your neck
breathe a sigh of relief
bright and early
bright-eyed and bushy-tailed
bright future
bring home the bacon
bring to a head
bring up the rear
briny deep
brown as a berry
bucking the trend
budding genius
buffeted by fate
bull by the horns

bundle of nerves
burning question
burn the midnight oil
burn your bridges
bury the hatchet
busman's holiday
busy as a bee
butter-and-egg man
butterflies in the stomach
by hook or crook
by the same token
by the skin of the teeth
by the sweat of his brow
callow youth
calm before the storm
can of worms
can't fight city hall
can't make head nor tail of
carry the ball
cart before the horse
cash on the barrel
cast bread upon the water
casting aspersions
cast the first stone
cast your lot with
cast your pearls before swine
caught red-handed
change your tune
checkered career
chip off the old block
clean as a whistle
clear as a bell
clear as crystal
clear as mud
clearing the decks
coals to Newcastle
cock-and-bull story
cold as ice
cold feet
cold sweat

come in out of the rain
come out in the wash
consensus of opinion
    (redundant as well as
    tiresome)
conspicuous by his absence
contents noted
cool as a cucumber
could care less
crack the whip
crash the gate
credibility gap
crooked as a dog's hind legs
crow to pick
crucial third-down situation
cry for the moon
cry over spilt milk
cry wolf
curiously enough (you don't
    need the *enough*)
cut the mustard
dead as a doornail
dead giveaway
deaf as a post
demon rum
depths of despair
devil to pay
diabolical plot
diamond in the rough
did a number
didn't know enough to come in
    out of the rain
didn't know from Adam
didn't lift a finger
die is cast
dirty old man
distance lends enchantment
distinguished speaker
don't put all your eggs in one
    basket

don't take any wooden nickels
doomed to disappointment
doting parent
down in the mouth
down my alley
draw the line
drink like a fish
drop in the bucket
drown his sorrow
drunk as a skunk
dull as dishwater (ditchwater)
dull thud
during the time that
dyed in the wool
each and every
eager beaver
early on
ear to the ground
easier said than done
eat, drink, and be merry
eat your hat
eleventh hour
enclosed please find
ends of the earth
everything went along nicely
exception proves the rule
explore every avenue
eyeball to eyeball
eyes bigger than one's stomach
eyes like saucers
eyes like stars
eyes of the world
face the music
fair and square
fair sex
far be it from me
far cry
fast and loose
fat's in the fire (a favorite of
    the late Erle Stanley

Gardner—he could get away
    with it)
feather in his cap
feel his oats
feet of clay
few and far between
few well-chosen words
field of endeavor
fill the bill
filthy lucre
fine and dandy
finger in every pie
first and foremost
first pop out of the box
fish or cut bait
fish out of water
flash in the pan
flat as a pancake
flat on your back
flip your lid
flog a dead horse
fly-by-night
fly in the ointment
fly off the handle
fond farewell
fools rush in
foregone conclusion
foreseeable future
for free
for the pure-and-simple reason
free gift
fresh as a daisy
fresh out of
from rags to riches
frozen stiff
frying pan into the fire
gainfully employed (you don't
    need the *gainfully*)
gala occasion
game plans

garden variety
gentle as a baby
gentle as a lamb
get in one's hair
get real
get the sack/shaft
get to the point
get your dander up
gild the lily
gird your loins
give a piece of your mind
give a wide berth
give me a break
give short shrift to
give the gate
glad rags
go against the grain
God's country
go hat in hand
gone to seed
good as gold
good as new
go on the warpath
goose that laid the golden egg
go scot-free
go the whole hog
got his number
go to pieces
go to the dogs
got the upper hand
got up on the wrong side of the
  bed
grain of salt
graphic account
great hue and cry
greatness thrust upon
green as grass
green with envy
grim reaper
grin like a Cheshire cat

ground below (Since the
  ground is usually below, you
  probably don't need to say
  below.)
gum up the works
had the privilege
hail-fellow-well-met
hair of the dog
hairbreadth
hair stand on end
halcyon days
hale and hearty
half a mind to
hammer and tongs
hand in glove
hand to mouth
handwriting on the wall
hang by a thread
hang in there, baby
happy as a lark
hard as nails
hard row to hoe
has a screw loose
has-been
HAVE A NICE DAY
have another think coming
haven't seen you in a coon's
  age
head above water
head and shoulders above
head over heels
heart in my mouth
heart in the right place
heart of gold
heart of hearts
hem and haw
herculean task
hide your light under a bushel
high-handed
high on the hog

hit below the belt
hit the nail on the head
hit the sack
hit your head against a stone wall
hold a candle to
hold the bag
hold the phone
hold your horses
hold your peace
holier than thou
hook, line, and sinker
hook or crook
hornet's nest
horns of a dilemma
horse of a different color
hungry as a bear
hurling invectives
I can't believe I ate the whole thing
if and when
if the shoe fits
if you follow me
ignorance is bliss
I'll buy that
I'll drink to that
in a pleasing manner
in a tight spot
in cahoots with
in conclusion would state
in full swing
in my judgment
in no uncertain terms
in one ear and out the other
in one fell swoop
in other words
in our midst (incorrect and misquoted—see Matthew 18:20)
inspiring sight

in spite of the fact that
institution of higher learning
interesting to note
intestinal fortitude
in the final/last analysis
in the know
in the light of
in the long run
in the midst of
in the same boat
in this day and age
in touch with
irons in the fire
irony of fate
it depends on whose ox is being gored
it goes without saying
it's a whole new ball game
it stands to reason
jog my memory
Johnny-on-the-spot/come lately
joined together
join the club
jumping-off place
jump the gun
jump to conclusions
just bear with me
just to inform you
keep a stiff upper lip
keep body and soul together
keep the ball rolling
keep the pot boiling
keep your eye on the ball
keep your eyes peeled
kick in the teeth
kill the fatted calf
kill two birds with one stone
know the ropes
labor of love

lady of leisure
land-office business
last but not least
last straw
law unto herself
lead-pipe cinch
lean-and-hungry look
lean over backward
leap in the dark
leave in the lurch
leave no stone unturned
left-handed compliment
legend in his own time
let it all hang out
let's face it
let the cat out of the bag
let your hair down
level with me
lick into shape
light as a feather
like a bump on a log
like a lead balloon
limp as a rag
lips sealed
little did I think when
little old lady
lit up like a Christmas tree
live and let live
live high off the hog
live in hopes that
live it up
live off the fat of the land
loaded for bear
lock, stock, and barrel
long arm of the law
long time no see
look a gift horse in the mouth
lose your marbles
lose your shirt
lot of laughs

lucky stiff
lump in the throat
mad as a wet hen
make a clean breast of it
make a long story short/make
    a long story longer
make a mountain out of a
    molehill
make a pitch
make ends meet
make hay while the sun shines
make it perfectly clear
make my day
make short work of
make the air blue
make the rounds (unless you're
    a doctor)
make things hum
master of all he surveys
may be favored
mean no offense
meets the eye
meets with your approval
method in his madness
might and main
mind your p's and q's
misery loves company
missed the boat
moment of truth
momentous decision
moot point
moot question
more easily said than done
more sinned against than
    sinning
more than meets the eye
more than she bargained for
more the merrier
motley crew
mute testimony

my bag
my door is always open
nagging headache
nail to the cross
naked truth
near at hand
near future
near miss
neat as a bandbox
necessary evil
neck and neck
neck of the woods
needle in a haystack
needless to say
needs no introduction
neither fish nor fowl
neither rhyme nor reason
never a dull moment
never in the history of
never too late
new broom sweeps clean
new lease on life
new wine in old bottles
nipped in the bud
nitty-gritty
no expense has been spared
no great shakes
no leg to stand on
no man in his right mind
none the worse for wear
no place like home
no reflection on you, but
no respecter of persons
nose out of joint
nose to the grindstone
no skin off my nose
no strings attached
not a leg to stand on
not by a long shot
nothing succeeds like success

nothing to sneeze at
nothing ventured
not to be sneezed at
not to exceed
not wisely but too well
not worth a Continental
not worth the paper it's written
   on
no way
nth degree
number is up
of a high order
off the record
of the first order
of the first water
old as Methuselah
old as the hills
old before his time
old head on young shoulders
old stomping/stamping ground
on a roll
on bended knee
on cloud nine
one and only
one and the same
on Easy Street
one foot in the grave
on his last legs
on pins and needles
on the fence
on the level
on the mark
on the ragged edge
on the spot
on top of the world
opportunity knocks but once
other fish to fry
other side of the coin
ours is not to reason why
out in left field

out of sight, out of mind
out of sorts
out of the mouths of babes
out of the woods
over a barrel
over the hill
ox to the slaughter
package solutions
pain in the neck
painting the town
pale as a ghost
part and parcel
pass the buck
pass the time of day
pave the way for
pay the piper
peer group
penny for your thoughts
period of time
perish the thought
personal growth
pet peeve
Philadelphia lawyer
picture of health
piece of your mind
pillar of society
pillar to post
pinch hitter
pin it on her/him
pipe dream
plan your work and work your
   plan
play a waiting game
play both ends against the
   middle
play fast and loose
play into the hands of
play it by ear
play to the grandstand
play up to

play with fire
play your cards right
point with pride
poor as a church mouse
power corrupts
powers that be
present company excepted
pretty as a picture
pretty kettle of fish
primrose path
protests too much
pull chestnuts from the fire
pull the wool over his/her eyes
pull up stakes
pull your leg
pull your own weight
pull yourself together
pure and simple
pure as the driven snow
put a bug in his ear
put on the dog
put on your thinking cap
put our heads together
put that in your pipe and
   smoke it
put the bite on
putty in his/her hands
put-up job
put your cards on the table
put your foot down
put your foot in it
put your foot in your mouth
put your hand to the plow
put your shoulder to the wheel
quick as a bunny
quick as a flash
quick as a wink
rack and ruin
rack your brain
raining cats and dogs

raise the dead
raise your sights
rake over the coals
ran circles around
rank has its privileges
rattle the wrong cage
read between the lines
read him/her like a book
read my lips
read the riot act
really and truly
red as a beet
red-carpet treatment
rich as Croesus
rich beyond my wildest dreams
ride the gravy train
ride roughshod over
right man in the right place
right on the head/money
right up my alley
ring a bell
ring true
ripe old age
rise to the occasion
roaring success
Rock of Gibraltar
roll out the red carpet
room at the top
rose-colored glasses
rough and ready
rough and tumble
round of applause
rub the wrong way
run for your money
run-of-the-mill
run up a red flag
sacred cow
sad but true
sadder but wiser
sad to tell

sail under false colors
same the whole world over
same wavelength
save for a rainy day
save your breath
save your own skin
sawdust trail
school of hard knocks
seal his doom
sea of faces
see a man about a dog
see beyond the nose on her
    face
seek his fortune
seek his own level
see my way clear
see the light of day
see what I mean
self-made man
sell him a bill of goods
sell like hotcakes
senior citizens (this has some
    defenders)
set teeth on edge
set the world on fire
set up shop
set your cap for
set your heart upon
seventh heaven
shadow of a doubt
shadow of his/her former self
shake a leg
shake a stick at
shake in my boots
shape of things to come
share these thoughts/words
shed a little light on the subject
ships that pass in the night
shoot the breeze
shoot the works

short and sweet
shot in the arm
shoulder to the wheel
sibling rivalry
sick and tired
sigh of relief
sight for sore eyes
sight to behold
sight unseen
sign of the times
silence is golden
silent as the grave
since time immemorial
single most
sing like a bird
sink or swim
sitting pretty
sixes and sevens
six of one and half dozen of
    the other
skate on thin ice
skin alive
skin and bones
skin deep
skirt around the edge of
slowly but surely
small world
smart money
smelled like a rose
snake in the grass
snowed under
soft as snow
soft shoulder to cry on
soft spot in his/her heart
so help me, Hannah
some kind of
something else
something's rotten in Denmark
so sue me
sound the trumpets

sow wild oats
spanner in the works
split hairs
spread yourself too thin
square meal
square peg in a round hole
square your conscience
stand on your own two feet
stand your ground
start from scratch
staying power
steal a march
steal your thunder
stick around awhile
stick-in-the-mud
stick in your craw
stick to the ribs
stick to your guns
stick your neck out
stiff-necked
stiff upper lip
still waters run deep
stock in trade
straight and narrow
straight as an arrow
straight from the horse's mouth
straight from the shoulder
strange as it seems
strange but true
strangely enough (just
    strangely will do)
straw in the wind
street of dreams
strike it rich
strike while the iron is hot
strike your fancy
string along with
strong as an ox
struck dumb
stubborn as a mule

stuff and nonsense
stuffed shirt
subsequent to
sum and substance
sumptuous repast
sun drenched
supreme sacrifice
sweeten the kitty
swing a deal
tables are turned
take a back seat
take a leaf out of one's book
take a shine to
take care
take it lying down
take stock in
take the liberty
take to his heels
take words out of his mouth
talk through your hat
telling blow
tell it to the marines
tell me about it
tender mercies
that is to say
that's it in a nutshell
the best-laid plans
the foreseeable future
the proud possessor
there's a method in his
  madness
there you go
the wheels of the gods grind
  slowly
the whole ball of wax
thick as thieves
thick- thin-skinned
thin as a rail
think tank
this side of the grave

those with whom we come in
  contact
through thick and thin
throw a wrench in the
  machinery
throw in the sponge
throw in the towel
throw the book at
tidy sum
time hangs heavy
time immemorial
time is of the essence
time was ripe
tiny tots
tired as a dog
tired but happy
tit for tat
to all intents and purposes
toe the mark
to gird up one's loins
to make a long story short
tongue in cheek
too funny for words
too many irons in the fire
too numerous to mention
tooth and nail
top drawer
to play ball with
to string along
to tell the truth
to the bitter end
to the manner born
touch with a ten-foot pole
tough act to follow
tough as nails
tower of strength
tread lightly
trials and tribulations
trip the light fantastic
true blue

true facts (facts are true)
try men's souls
truth to tell
turnabout is fair play
turn a cold shoulder
turn a deaf ear
turn a hand
turn back the clock
turn over a new leaf
turn the other cheek
turn the tables
turn thumbs down
turn up your nose
two strings to your bow
ugly as sin
ugly duckling
unable to see the forest for the
   trees
undercurrent of excitement
under the wire
uneasy truce
unless and until
untiring efforts
up against it
ups and downs
value system
vast concourse
view with alarm
virtual standstill
viselike grip
wait on hand and foot
walk a tightrope
walks of life
warm as toast
warm the cockles of one's
   heart
wash one's dirty linen in public
wash one's hands of it
water under the bridge

water over the dam
way out
way to go
weaker sex
wear and tear
weather eye open
wee small hours
wended their way
whipping boy
white as a sheet
wide of the mark
wide open spaces
wild oats
wind out of your sails
win your spurs
wishy-washy
with a high hand
with all my heart
with a vengeance
with bated breath
without a doubt
without a prayer
without rhyme or reason
wolf from the door
wolf in sheep's clothing
wonderful world of . . .
word to the wise
world is his oyster
worse for wear
worthy opponent
would I lie to you?
wreathed in smiles
wrong end of the stick
yellow-bellied
YOU KNOW
you'd better believe it
your guess is as good as mine
your kind indulgence
you've come a long way, baby

Reprinted by permission of Johnny Hart and Creators Syndicate.

2

USAGE

Once you have removed the static from your communications system by eliminating all the words that are wrong, you can then improve your image even further by following these two rules:

1. *Don't be afraid to use the correct word. It may sound a little stilted to you, or strange, but most of the strangeness is due to the fact that you haven't used the word before. Or if you have, you haven't used it correctly. Don't avoid the word; learn its meaning and then use it.*

2. *Never lower your standards to match those people around you by using errors in your own speech.*

aggravate   "To make worse, to increase," as in **to aggravate a condition.** Do not use when you mean **irritate** or **annoy. I am irritated** rather than *I am aggravated.*

agree to, agree with   You **agree to** a plan or suggestion and **agree with** a person. One thing **agrees with** another thing.

almost   "Not quite." Do not say *most* for **almost. Almost everybody was there.**

alternative   Some careful speakers and writers insist that there can be only two **alternatives** in any situation. If there are more, they become **choices** or **possibilities.** Some say that if you *have* to choose one of them, they are **alternatives,** no matter how many there are.

among Use **among** when referring to three or more items. Use **between** if there are only two. **Between you and me. Among the three of us.** In very rare instances, **between** may be proper with more than two, as when the action described can only take place between two of the several at one time.

amount Use **amount** to refer to a general quantity. **There was a large amount of work to be done.** Use **number** to refer to items that can be counted.

and Do not use this word when you mean **to,** for example, **come to see me,** not *come and see me.* See TRY AND.

angry One is angry **at** a situation but angry **with** a person.

anxious "To be worried, apprehensive." Do not confuse with **eager,** wanting something very much.

anyplace Careful speakers and writers avoid this term as a substitute for **anywhere.** In sentences such as **We couldn't find any place to park,** it is two words.

as "Equally, in the same manner." **As** is correct before a phrase. **She thinks as I do.** Do not substitute *like,* which is used before nouns or pronouns. See LIKE.

at This word should not be used at the end of a sentence starting with **where.** Say **Where is the book?** not *Where is the book at?*

author This is a noun, not a verb. Instead of saying *She authored the book,* say **She is the author of the book.**

barely   Guard against using with other negative words, as **barely** is already negative, and two negatives cancel each other. Say **can barely,** not *can't barely.*

basis   Remember that the plural form is **bases,** pronounced **bay'·seez.**

beside   "At the side of, alongside." Do not use *of* after it. **The chair is beside the desk.** Compare with BESIDES.

besides   "In addition to, as well as." **He has plenty to do besides study.**

be sure and   **Be sure to** is the correct form.

between   Say **between you and me,** never *between you and I.* See also AMONG.

biweekly   This tricky word can mean "twice a week" or "every two weeks," so we never know what to believe when we see or hear it. In your own speech, it's better to use **biweekly** for "every two weeks" and **semiweekly** for "twice a week."

boat   "A small vessel." An ocean liner, or any other big vessel, is not a *boat* but a **ship.**

both alike   Say simply **they are alike.** You don't need the *both.*

boy   Do not use to refer to a man.

bring   In the sense of conveying, **bring** indicates movement toward the speaker. Example: **Bring the book to me.** The sentence *Bring this form when you go to the doctor's office* is wrong. The word should be **take.** See TAKE.

but   This word is not needed after *doubt* and *help.* Say **I don't doubt that** rather than *I don't doubt but that.*

check into, check out   Usually **check** is sufficient. You do, of course, **check into** your hotel and go to the **checkout** counter.

claim	This word is not to be used as a substitute for **say.** Wrong: *She claimed I did it.* Right: **She said I did it.**
class	Do not use this word to describe style (it shows a lack of it). *She really has class* shows that the speaker has none.
come	Do not use this word instead of **came.** The past tense of *come* is came. **I came to the party early.**
come and	Say **come to: Come to see me tomorrow.**
compare with, compare to	**Compare with** is used with two things or people of equal stature, perhaps to point out differences. **Compare to** means "liken to" and is used for fanciful comparisons: **"Shall I compare thee to a summer's day?"** Or: **He compared his teacher to Socrates.**
comptroller	A variant of the word **controller.** Used as the title for a financial officer. Pronounce the same as **controller.**
convince	**Convince** is used with **of** or **that.** Avoid using with *to.* One may persuade someone to do something—in fact, **persuade** can be used with all three constructions.
couple	We need to exercise care in the pluralization of this word. Say two couples, not *two couple.*
crass	The original and still preferred meaning here is "stupid." The word sounds like **brassy, gross,** and **crude,** but these are very new meanings.
criterion, criteria	A **criterion** is a standard test by which something is compared or measured. The plural is **criteria,** often used incorrectly as the singular.
datum, data	The word **datum,** rarely used, means a "fact." The plural form is **data.** Although **data** is widely used for both the

singular and plural, it is comforting to know the difference.

decimate   This is from the Latin *decem,* "ten." It means, literally, to "select by lot and kill one in every ten." Many people use it incorrectly to mean "the killing of a large number," or "total destruction."

did, done   Avoid *I have did.* Say simply, **I did.** The word **have** must be followed by **done,** as in **I have done my work.** Likewise, never say *I done.*

differ   **Differ with** a person; **differ from** something; **differ on** an issue.

different   **Different from** is the correct form. *Different than* is to be avoided, although **other than** is all right.

discover   Do not use interchangeably with **invent. Discover** means "to learn of "; **invent** means "to originate."

disinterested   "Impartial, objective." A judge should be a **disinterested** listener. (He should not take sides.) If you mean "having no interest in," say **uninterested. He was an uninterested student; he did a lot of day-dreaming.**

distrust   "Lack of trust." It has the same meaning as **mistrust.**

done   Not interchangeable with **finish.** If you say **The painting will be done next week,** it is unclear whether you mean "someone will be painting next week" or "by next week the painting will be completed."

draught   Chiefly British. Pronunciation and meaning identical to **draft.**

drug   This is not the past tense of **drag.** Say **dragged. She dragged the child out of the room.**

each	A singular word. When used in a sentence it must be matched with other singular words. Say **each brought his own** (not *their own*). Since **their** is plural, it is correctly used as follows: **They brought their own.** The plural **their** matches the plural **they.**
eager	"Desirous of something." Do not confuse with **anxious.**
end product	Just say **product** (unless you need to distinguish something from an intermediate product).
enough	Guard against inserting *enough* when it is not needed. *We were fortunate enough to receive the gift* is strengthened by saying simply **We were fortunate to receive the gift.**
et cetera	Never say *and et cetera. Et* is Latin for **and.**
everybody . . . their	**Everybody** is still singular and takes a singular pronoun: **Everybody had his or her own umbrella at last.** If that elaborate **his or her** bothers you, say **We all had our own** or **They all had their own.**
everyplace	Not when you mean **everywhere.** In sentences such as **Every place was taken,** it is two words.
except	You'll do all right if you remember to use **me, him,** and **her** after **except,** in sentences such as **No one loved you except me,** and, similarly, **No one loves him except her.**
feel	When used as a substitute for **think** or **believe,** make sure it fits the context better, and you are not using it just to hedge.
female	When referring to human beings, do not use this word as a noun. You may refer

to a **group of women,** but not to a *group of females.* It is all right to refer to animals as **females.**

fewer An adjective meaning "a smaller number." Say **There are fewer children in school,** not *there are less children.* See LESS.

fit The past tense of this verb is **fitted.**

flammable, inflammable **Flammable** and **inflammable** are the same in usage and meaning. See NON-FLAMMABLE. (One oil company avoids the problems by putting COMBUSTIBLE on the sides of its trucks.)

foot/feet It is all right to say **a six-foot rug.** But a man is **six feet tall,** not *six foot.*

former Use **former** to refer to the first of two things. Use **first** to refer to the first of more than two things. **Nicky Hilton was Elizabeth Taylor's first husband.**

froze Do not say *I am froze.* Say either **I froze** or **I am frozen.**

gal Many women are campaigning against the use of the word *gal.* **Woman** is preferred.

gift By definition, a gift is free. Do not say *a free gift.*

girl Do not use the word **girl** to refer to a woman.

give The past tense of this word is **gave. I gave it to him yesterday.** Never, never say *I have gave.* When paired with **have,** the correct form is **given. I have given it to him.**

good/well Instead of getting into the *I feel good/I feel well* dilemma, say **I am well.** It's easier.

got Do not use when you mean **have.** Wrong: *I got my book with me.* Right: **I have my book with me.**

graduate	You can **graduate from a school** or **be graduated from a school.** You cannot *graduate it,* however, unless you have been given the responsibility of dividing it into grades. *He graduated high school* shows that the speaker probably did not.
grammatical	"According to the rules of grammar." Accordingly, we don't say *grammatical errors* but, rather, **errors in grammar.**
hanged	A man is **hanged.** A picture is **hung.**
hardly	Guard against using with other negative words; **hardly** is already negative. And two negatives cancel each other. Say **can hardly,** not *can't hardly.*
home	Not to be used interchangeably with **house.** The latter refers to a dwelling. Sometimes a **home** can be created there.
human	Pronounced **hyoo'•mun,** this is an adjective, often describing the word **being,** as in **human being.** *Human* as a noun is common only in science fiction. (Sound the **h.**)
I	Use **I** only as the subject of a sentence (**I like this**) or after **is** and **was** (**It is I**).
I been	The correct way to say this is **I have been.**
index	The preferred plural form of this word is **indexes,** except in mathematics, where **indices** is common.
individual	Should not be used indiscriminately for "person." **Person** may be applied to anyone as a general term. An individual is a particular being.
infamous	Pronounced **in'•fa•mus,** this word means "disgraceful, having a bad reputation." It does not mean *unknown.*
innovation	Do not put *new* in front of this word: If something is **innovative,** it is new.

invaluable "Too valuable to be measured." Do not use when you mean **valuable.**

invent "To originate something." Compare with DISCOVER.

invite A verb. Do not use as a noun; that is, you receive an **invitation,** not an *invite.*

join together, joined together Just say **join.** You don't need to add *together.* (The use of **join together** *is* acceptable in marriage ceremonies.)

kind Say **that kind** or **those kinds.** Do not say *those kind.*

knot This word has several meanings, one of which is "a unit of speed." The words *an hour* should never follow it. A ship can travel at six knots or at six nautical miles per hour, but *not* at *six knots per hour.*

kudos Pronounced **koo′•dahs** or **koo′•dos.** This Greek word means "glory or fame." The final **s** is not the sign of a plural: No such thing exists as *a kudo.* **Kudos** is singular: **Kudos was due the first astronaut.**

lay/lie In the present tense, the verb **lay** needs an object: **Hens lay eggs. Lay the book on the table.** Lay is also the *past* tense of the verb **lie,** meaning "to assume a reclining position." **I want to lie down. Please lie down. Let's lie out in the sun. I lay down yesterday.** (If the verb **lie** refers to the telling of a falsehood, the past tense is **lied,** as in **He lied to me.**)

learn Do not use *learn* when you mean **teach.** A student learns. A teacher teaches. You cannot *learn* someone how to do something, but you can **teach** him.

leave This word usually means "to depart." **Leave without me.** Do not confuse it with the word **let,** which usually means "to permit." Correct: **Let it stand the way it is. Let go of me.** But not *Leave go of me.*

legalistic Not interchangeable with **legal. Legalistic** implies a stricter application to the law than does **legal.**

lend As a verb this word is preferred over **loan.** The latter has been established as a verb in business usage; however, it is still preferable to keep the forms separate. **She asked her father for a loan, and he lent her the amount she needed.**

less An adjective or an adverb meaning "not so much." **There is less milk left than I thought.** Say **fewer** when you refer to something that can be counted. See FEWER.

liable Pronounced **li'•u•bl,** this word means "legally responsible, or probable—in the sense of something impending, usually dangerous or unpleasant." **Reckless motorists are liable to suffer injuries.** Do not use as a substitute for *likely.*

like "Equally, in the same manner." Use **like** before nouns or pronouns. Do not substitute *as,* which is used before a phrase or clause. See AS.

likely "Probable." **The moon is likely to come out tonight.** The word has no negative connotation, as does *liable.*

lines of communication Usually preferred over *line* of *communications.*

lit The latest dictionaries sanction this usage as a past-tense form of **to light,** although **lighted** remains the more accepted form. **Lit** is all right when used as a participle: **The candles are lit.**

livid "Bluish," as in a **livid** bruise.

loan See LEND.

loath/loathe **Loath** means unwilling. **Loathe** means to hate or abhor. **He was loath to have dinner with her after their quarrel. He loathed the very idea.**

lots of **Many** is preferred.

mad **Mad** means "crazy or frenzied." Do not use when you mean **angry.**

male Do not use as a noun. **Male** is acceptable as a noun only with reference to animals.

maltreat, mistreat These two words are interchangeable.

man Be aware that terms such as *postman, mailman, policeman,* etc., are considered passé and even sexist. Use **people** or **person** or the appropriate new term, for example, **letter carrier** for *mailman.*

me Use it with confidence. Do not substitute **I** as the object of a verb or preposition. Say **between you and me. They came to see Bruce and me.** Do not use **me** as a subject. It is incorrect to say *Me and John are going* or *John and me are going.*

media This is the plural of **medium.** Say **Radio and television are popular media.** But **Radio remains a popular medium.** When **medium** refers to someone with psychic abilities, the plural is **mediums.**

mile It is all right to say **one mile,** but with two or more miles it is necessary to add that **s.** One may refer to a **ten-mile drive.** But do not say *I live ten mile from here.*

most Do not substitute for **almost.** The misuse of *most* for **very** occurs more often in written than in spoken English, but beware of sentences such as *He was* *most cooperative,* when "he" is not being compared with anyone.

my Possessive case of the pronoun **I.** Say **This is my book.** Also say **He objected to my going.** Do not say *Do you mind me going without you?*"

myself You can use this word to refer *back* to yourself (**I dressed myself**) or for emphasis (**I'd rather do it myself.**) When it is incorrectly used, it hurts many ears. Wrong: *He asked Bruce and myself.* Say **He asked Bruce and me.** Wrong: *Bruce and myself are undecided.*

never Means "not ever." Do not use when you mean **not.** *Who spilled the milk? I never did it!* implies that you have never in your life spilled milk.

none Means "no one." Say **None of us is ready. None** is a singular subject. It demands a singular verb to match.

nonflammable Since **flammable** and **inflammable** are interchangeable, use **nonflammable** to mean "will not burn."

not only . . . but also If you use this construction, all four words must be used, and the sentence should be constructed so that **not** and **only** fall together and **but** and **also** fall together. **You prove yourself to be not only well educated but also a clear thinker when you use this construction properly.**

number Use **number** to refer to items that can be counted; use **amount** to refer to a general quantity. **A number of people were present. I need a large amount of sugar.** See AMOUNT.

of Not a substitute for **have.** Do not say *I would of gone,* or *I wish I could of been* *there,* or *you shouldn't of said that.* It is **would have, could have, should have.** Also, it is redundant to add the word *of* after such words as *outside, off,* or *inside.*

only   Pay attention to where you place this word in your sentences. Example: *I only arrived yesterday* is probably incorrect unless the **only** thing you did yesterday was arrive. What you probably mean is **I arrived only yesterday.**

oral   Oral means "spoken." It is not interchangeable with **verbal. Verbal** can mean "spoken" or it can refer to something that is written.

other than   Not *different than,* although you may say **different from.**

out   With **hide, win,** and **lose,** *out* is superfluous.

over   Instead of saying *Over forty members were there,* say **More than forty members were there.**

over with   Omit the *with.*

pair, pairs   The plural of **pair** is **pairs. I plan to take two pairs of shoes.** Never say *two pair.*

party   Usually refers to more than one person. Exceptions: telephone and legal usage.

peer   In Britain a **peer** is a nobleman. But in this country a **peer** is one who has equal standing with another. Do not use when you refer to a superior.

phase   Means "state of transition or development." It is not to be used to mean *aspect* or *topic.*

phenomena   This is the plural of **phenomenon,** "a visible occurrence or one that is extraordinary or marvelous." Do not use **phenomena** when speaking of only one such occurrence.

pimento, pimiento Both spellings are acceptable, and both are pronounced **pi•men'•to.**

preventative **Preventive** is preferred. Many Cincinnati doctors swear there was once a University of Cincinnati professor of preventive medicine who would flunk a student who said *preventative.*

proved As the past tense of **prove,** preferred over *proven.* **It has been proved.** It is acceptable to use **proven** as an adjective: **a proven fact.**

provided Preferred over *providing* when used to mean "on the condition that." **We will go provided it doesn't rain.**

quarter of, quarter to When referring to time, it is correct to say **a quarter to three.** In the case of money one says **a quarter of a dollar.**

quash "To put down or suppress completely." Not to be used in a milder sense. **The revolution was quashed.**

quick An adjective meaning "speedy." It is not acceptable to most experts when used as an adverb. They cringe if they see or hear *Come quick.* Add the **-ly** to make it right.

refined This word should not be used to describe people. Sugar is **refined.**

regard "To consider." **Regard** also means "to hold in high esteem." It can be used to mean "reference," as in **with regard to your question.** *With regards to* is incorrect.

regards "Greetings." This word is not considered to be interchangeable with **respect** (in the sense of **with respect to**). Nor is it interchangeable with **regard.**

relator A **relator** narrates an account or story. Do not use when you mean **Realtor,** a real estate agent affiliated with the National Association of Real Estate Boards. (Not all real estate agents are Realtors.)

rob He *robbed my pencil* is bad English. A person can be **robbed,** but his possessions are **stolen.**

run The past tense is **ran. I ran yesterday,** not *I run yesterday.* However, it is correct to say **I have run.**

sanatarium "A health resort." The word **sanatorium,** which used to refer to a mental institution, now can have the same meaning as **sanatarium;** however, it should be noted that there is still an aura of the old meaning hovering around **sanatorium.**

saw One should not put *have* in front of this word. Say **I saw,** not *I have saw.* Also correct: **I have seen.** See SEEN.

scarcely Avoid using with another negative word, as **scarcely** is already negative, and two negatives cancel each other out. Say **can scarcely,** not *can't scarcely.* Say **I can scarcely,** rather than *I can't scarcely.*

scissors Plural in form and used with a plural verb. We usually refer to **a pair of scissors.** Also, **Where are the scissors?**

seen Avoid saying *I seen.* It is **I have seen** or **I saw.** See SAW.

should of Incorrect way of saying **should have.**

simultaneous Do not use to describe an action but only to describe a thing or things. It is a **simultaneous occurrence** if two things happen simultaneously.

sinus Something everybody has—so do not announce that you *have sinus.* You probably mean that you are having **sinus inflammation** or **sinus discomfort.**

strata	The plural form of **stratum.** It means "layers." You may refer to **every stratum of society,** but you would say **all strata of society.**
suite	Pronounced **sweet.** It means "a succession of related things: a series of connected rooms; a matched set of furniture." Please note: You may have a **suit** of clothes, but you own a **suite** of furniture.
suspicion	If you suspect something, you have a **suspicion.** Do not say *I suspicion.*
swum	The past tense of **I swim** is **I swam,** or you may say **I have swum.** You may also use **swum** when speaking of distance **to be swum.**
take	Use **take** to indicate movement away from the speaker. Example: **Take the book to him.** Compare with BRING.
temperature	**Tem′•pur•ah•chur.** The degree of hotness or coldness. Since everybody has one, it sounds a bit naive to announce brightly, *I have a temperature.* If you want to tell us about it, report on whether it is above or below normal. Or simply say **I have a fever.**
tract	Do not say *tract* when you mean **track.**
transpire	Careful writers do not use *transpire* when they mean **happen** or **come to pass. Transpire** means "to be revealed, to become known," as in **We had to wait until after the war for the secret to transpire.**
trivia	Plural. It is wrong to say, *I don't enjoy talking about this trivia,* and *these trivia* sounds stilted. **These trivial matters** is all right. But if it's the what's-the-name-of-Buck-Rogers's-horse variety you're talking about, you're better off keeping

	away from all words that require a singular or plural form. No one ever says *a trivium,* either.
try and	Say **try to** rather than *try and;* for example, **Try to come along.** See AND.
undersigned	This word seems stuffy to most people, but it is perfectly acceptable, so use it where indicated—usually only in written legal documents or other official letters or agreements.
unique	Means "the only one of its kind." It is incorrect to say *most unique* or *very unique.*
up	This is standard English, but it frequently **turns up** when not needed. Words such as **add, head, start, think,** and **wait** are stronger when you don't put *up* after them. It doesn't belong before **until** either.
utilize	To **utilize** something is to "find use for something already in service or to expand productivity by finding new uses." Do not substitute **utilize** for **use** if it does not have one of these meanings.
valuable	"Having value." Compare with INVALUABLE.
via	The meaning is usually restricted to "by way of," rather than "by means of."
virus	You can't *have a virus* the way you **have a cold.** A virus is smaller than a germ, and when you're ill with a virus attack, you may have more than one virus.
wait on	Do not use when you mean **wait for.** A valet may **wait on** his master, but you do not *wait on* a friend unless you are serving him. Say **I am waiting for him.**
way	Take care to say **a way** when your meaning is singular: **Phyllis has a long**

	way to go. Add the s only when you refer to more than one way: **There are two ways to look at it.**
went	*Have* should never appear in front of **went. I went,** or **I have gone.**
wore out	It is all right to say **I wore out my shoes.** It is not acceptable to say *I'm wore out.* Say **I'm worn out,** or, better still, **I'm tired.**
would	Almost everyone deplores the use of *would of* for **would have,** and of *if he would have* for **if he had.**
wrench	"A tool." Or, if used as a verb, it means to "twist violently." It does not mean to "rinse."
Xmas	Although **X** represents the Greek letter **chi,** a symbol for Christ, this abbreviation is offensive to some Christians.
yet	Use only when it increases the clarity of a sentence; avoid the unnecessary *yet.* It is better to say **Have you washed?** than *Have you washed yet?*
yourself	**Yourself** is not interchangeable with **you.** It is right to say **I plan to invite Gloria and you,** and wrong to say *I plan to invite Gloria and yourself.* See MYSELF.

UNMATCHED PAIRS

Many of these word couples have nothing in common but their sound, whereas some are similar in meaning but not identical. Learn to distinguish them and you will have found another way of improving your spoken English.

abjure/adjure	To **abjure** something is to "repudiate or renounce" it. **Adjure** means "command or entreat."

adverse/averse   **Adverse** means "detrimental in design or effect": **The medication caused an adverse reaction. Averse** means "strongly disinclined."

advice/advise   One offers **advice** (noun) when one **advises** (verb).

affect/effect   **Affect** means to "influence." The result is an **effect. Effect** is also a verb meaning "to bring about; cause." (By the way, there is a noun **affect** in psychology, meaning a "feeling or emotion." It is pronounced with the accent on the first syllable.)

allude/elude   **Allude** means "refer obliquely." **Elude** means to "evade."

allusion/illusion   An **allusion** is an indirect reference. Don't confuse with **illusion:** "an unreal image, a false impression." And never use **allusion** for a direct reference; just say **reference.**

alternately/alternative   To **alternate** is to "go back and forth between two things"; thus, **alternately** means "as an occasional substitute." An **alternative** is an "option," and is the proper word to introduce a second, or even third, possibility. See ALTERNATIVE in Usage section.

assure/ensure   To **assure** is "to state with confidence that something has been or will be accomplished." To **ensure** is to "make certain of something." (**Insure** is reserved for the insurance-company kind of **insure.**)

avenge/revenge   To **avenge** means to "exact justice." It is often confused with the word **revenge,** which means to "retaliate." If you will remember that **revenge** and **retaliate** both start with **re-,** you won't have any more trouble with these words. The corresponding nouns are **vengeance** and **revenge.**

beside/besides   **Beside** means "at the side of, alongside." Do not use *of* after the word **beside. Besides** means "in addition to, as well as."

biannual/biennial   The first means "twice a year" and is interchangeable with **semiannual.** The second means "every two years."

Calvary/cavalry   **Calvary** is the place near Jerusalem where Christ was crucified. **Cavalry** has to do with horses. I always remember the distinction between these two by associating **Calvin,** the Christian reformer, with the first and the word **cavalier** with the second.

cement/concrete   The first is dry; the second is first wet and then dry. **Concrete** is a mixture of **cement,** sand, gravel, and water.

censor/censure   A **censor** is "one who examines or judges." As a verb, **censor** means to "examine or assess." A **censure** is an "expression of disapproval." As a verb, it means "to express disapproval."

charted/chartered   **Charted** means mapped out. **Chartered** means either certified or hired/rented for your exclusive but temporary use.

childish/childlike   **Childish** means "of, similar to, or suitable for a child." When used to describe an adult, the word often connotes foolishness. **Childlike** is a more positive word, meaning "like, or befitting, a child; innocent."

climactic/climatic   **Climactic** means "pertaining to a climax." **Climatic** has to do with conditions of climate.

collaborate/corroborate   Keep in mind that the word **labor** is contained in **collaborate** and you'll re-

member that it means "work together."
To **corroborate** is to "confirm or
strengthen." **He corroborated her testimony.**

comprise/constitute **Comprise** means "embrace"—there's a
vivid image for you. Remember it and
you'll never say *the seven people who
comprise the committee.* They **constitute**
it. Or, **The committee comprises seven
members.**

connive/contrive **Connive** originally meant (and in precise
usage still means) to "shut one's eyes to
a crime." Possibly by confusion with
contrive, it has come to be misused for
the perpetration of the crime itself. The
right word to use for a criminal act involving plotting is **conspire.**

contemptible/ **Contemptible** means "deserving of con-
contemptuous tempt"; **contemptuous** means "having
contempt for."

continual/continuous **Continual** means "again and again";
continuous, "without interruption."

credible/credulous **Credible** means "believable." **Credulous**
means "gullible, ready to believe."
(**Creditable** has nothing to do with be-
lieving; it means "deserving of credit or
praise.")

deprecate/depreciate **Deprecate** is often misused for **depreciate. Deprecate** means "to seek to avert
by supplication," or "to disapprove."
To **depreciate** is to "lower in value."
The phrase *self-deprecating remarks* is
best altered to **self-belittling** or **self-dis-
paraging remarks.**

discreet/discrete When we show good judgment we are
discreet, or prudent. Something is **dis-
crete** if it is a separate, unconnected en-
tity.

disinterested/ uninterested	**Disinterested** implies an unbiased indifference. **Uninterested** is simple lack of interest, or apathy.
distrait/distraught	**Distrait,** pronounced **dis•trā′,** means "absentminded, inattentive." **Distraught** means "distracted, harassed."
elicit/illicit	To **elicit** is to "draw forth, to evoke." **Illicit** is an adjective meaning "illegal or unlawful."
emigrate/immigrate	Keep in mind that **immigrate** and **in** both start with an **i,** and you may remember that **immigrate** means "to go into a country"; **emigrate,** "to leave it."
eminent/imminent	**Eminent** means "high in station or esteem"; **imminent** means "about to happen."
farther/further	**Farther** refers to measurable distance. **Their house is farther away than we thought. Further,** as an adjective, describes "a continuation, usually of time or degree." **She had further news.** (As a verb it means "to advance," as in **to further a career.**)
faze/phase	**Faze** means to drive away or frighten. **Phase** usually refers to a cycle or a stage.
fiscal/physical	**Fiscal,** pronounced **fis′•kul,** means "of or pertaining to finance." **Physical, fiz′•u•kul,** means "pertaining to the body."
flair/flare	Some people have a **flair,** or aptitude, for art. A **flare** is a bright light or the act of burning brightly with sudden energy.
flaunt/flout	To **flaunt** is to "show off "; to **flout** is to "scorn, to scoff at, to show contempt for."
formally/formerly	**Formally** means "in a strict or formal manner"; **formerly** means "previously."

healthful/healthy   **Healthful** means "health-giving"; **healthy** means "possessing health." It is therefore erroneous to speak of a *healthy walk in the mountains* or *glass of milk*—these things are **healthful.**

historic/historical   **Historic** means "important or famous in history; having influence on history." **The walk on the moon was a historic event.** In contrast, **historical** means "based on history." You may speak of a **historical novel** or a **historical fact** but not a *historical occurrence.*

imply/infer   Speakers and writers **imply** something by what they say; they do not *infer*. The listeners or readers **infer** something from the remarks of the speakers or writers. Do not say *are you inferring?* when you mean **are you implying.**

important/importantly   Drop the *ly* when you use this as an adjective: "Most **important,** he had a degree in brain surgery."

impracticable/ impractical   **Impracticable** means "not capable of being carried out; unreasonably difficult of performance." Something that is **impractical** is "not a wise thing to implement or do."

ingenious/ingenuous   **Ingenious,** pronounced **in•jee′•nyus,** means "resourceful, clever, inventive, adroit." The slightly rarer **ingenuous, in•jen′•yoo•us,** means "frank, open, honest."

languishing/lavishing   The first means "fading away, growing weak," as in **He was languishing in the tropical climate. Lavishing** means "laying generously upon," often used with praise: **to lavish with praise.**

lightning/lightening   **Lightening** is a lessening of a burden. **Lightning** is the electrical phenomenon that occurs during a storm.

limp/limpid — Everyone knows what **limp** means. Beware of saying **limpid** for anything but "clear": **Her eyes were limpid jewels of blue.**

loose/lose — **Loose,** pronounced **loos,** means "not confined or restrained; free." To **lose,** pronounced **looz,** is to "mislay," or "not to win."

luxuriant/luxurious — The first means "overgrown, as a forest; full." The second, much more common, means "rich; elegant; commodious."

mantel/mantle — A **mantel** is the shelf above a fireplace. A **mantle** is a cloak.

marital/martial — **Marital,** pronounced **mair'•i•tul,** means "pertaining to marriage." **Martial** means "of war; suitable for war; warlike," and is pronounced **mahr'•shul.**

meantime/meanwhile — Remember the cliché "meanwhile, back at the ranch," and you won't confuse these two. **Meanwhile** is an adverb, a word used to describe an action; **meantime** is a noun. Therefore, you can't say *in the meanwhile* or *meantime, back at the ranch.*

moral/morale — **Moral,** "ethical, virtuous," is pronounced **maw'•rul. Morale, maw•ral',** means "the state of the spirits of an individual or group."

nauseated/nauseous — **Nauseated** means "feeling nausea"; **nauseous** means "causing nausea." **It was a nauseous situation.** Do not say *I feel nauseous;* rather, say **I am nauseated.**

noisome/noisy — **Noisome** means "offensive, particularly with reference to odors." Do not use it to mean "somewhat noisy."

partial/partly — **Partial** refers to preference. It is not interchangeable with **partly.**

peak/peek — When the cloud cover broke, we got a **peek** at the **peak** of the mountain.

persecute/prosecute Both words describe negative actions by one person toward another, but **persecute** means "to oppress, annoy, molest, bother." **Prosecute** means to "sue, indict, arraign, follow, pursue."

pore/pour **He pored** (not *poured*) **over the manuscript to make sure it was complete.**

prostate/prostrate The first is a gland. **Prostrate** means "stretched out, prone; powerless, resigned." By the way, don't confuse **prone** ("lying face down") with **supine** ("lying face up").

purposefully/purposely The first means "with purpose and determination"; the second, "intentionally."

ravage/ravish Both have something to do with violence, but **ravage** means "destroy" and **ravish** means "rape or violate."

regime/regimen **Regime** means "rule"; **regimen** means "routine." So you don't follow a *regime of diet and exercise;* it's a **regimen.**

regretfully/regrettably **Regretfully** describes the feeling of regret; **regrettably** expresses the fact that something is worthy of regret.

relevant/revelant **Relevant** means "pertinent," **revelant** is a nonword and should be excised.

rend/render To **rend** is to "tear." **Render** means to "give, deliver, impart; melt."

sensual/sexual **Sensual** refers to the senses—taste, feel, smell, sight, hearing—and their gratification. **Sexual** refers to sex and reproduction. **Sensuous** can refer to any of the senses but more often applies to those involved in aesthetic enjoyment of art, music, nature and the like.

straight/strait We sailed on a **straight** course through the dangerous **strait.**

tack/tact A **tack** is a short light nail with a sharp point. **Tact** is the ability to do or say the most diplomatic or fitting thing. They should *not* be pronounced the same way.

team/teem   A **team** is a group with a single goal. Something **teems,** or abounds, with life.

tortuous/torturous   **Tortuous:** "winding, twisting, circuitous," as in **It was a tortuous road. Torturous,** less frequently used, means "painful."

turbid/turgid   **Turbid** means "clouded; muddied." **Turgid** means "inflated, stiff."

venal/venial   **Venal** means "susceptible to bribery; corruptible." Do not confuse with **venial,** which, although it sometimes has to do with describing sin, means "excusable, pardonable."

wangle/wrangle   **Wangle** means "to get by contrivance; to manipulate." Do not confuse with **wrangle,** which means "to bicker; to herd horses or other livestock."

3

PRONUNCIATION
PITFALLS

Pronunciation is a difficult area of speech for most of us because we don't really listen to ourselves. "Proof-*heed*ing" our speech is every bit as tricky as proofreading something we've written.

Participants in my Word Watchers' Clinic assure me they have mastered pitfalls in pronunciation by following the suggestions below. You can too.

1. *Use the "buddy system." Ask your spouse (who probably has your errors on tap), a fellow student, a co-worker, your child, or a friend to help you spot your mistakes. Do the same for her or him if asked.*
2. *Read each pronunciation given here as though you had never seen the word before. Remember this is a special list. It consists of mispronunciations considered errors by the hundreds of contributors to this book.*
3. *If you have access to a tape recorder, by all means use it. Hear yourself as others do. Record the correct pronunciations of words that trouble you. Practice the pronunciation until you have mastered it. You can also record talk shows or educational material and play them back to make sure you have understood every word.*
4. *Check in an unabridged dictionary the pronunciation of each new word you hear.*

5. *Make flash cards of words you frequently mispro-nounce. Keep the cards with you until you can pro-nounce each word as automatically as you say "dog" and "cat."*

This chapter contains a list of words that are frequently mispronounced. Learn the ones that you have trouble with—and be honest. Then make it a lifetime habit to let no word go unturned; that is, turn those dictionary pages. Learn each new word and *practice* it until you're able to use it naturally. The rewards to your self-confidence will make it worthwhile.

Pronunciation Key

a	as in d*a*d	ī	as in b*i*te
ā	as in d*ay*	ō	as in *oa*t
ah	as in f*a*ther	oo	as in f*oo*l
ai	as in c*a*re	o͝o	as in l*oo*k
au	as in n*ow*	oi	as in b*oy*
aw	as in cr*o*ss	ur	as in h*er*
e	as in s*e*t	u	as in l*u*ck
ee	as in b*ee*t	j	as in *j*am
i	as in b*i*t	zh	as in vi*s*ion

absorb	**ab•sawrb′** is preferred over *ab•zawb′*.
absurd	"Contrary to common sense; lu-dicrous." It's pronounced **ab•surd′**, not *ab•zurd′*.
accessory	"Anything that contributes in a second-ary way," as **accessories** to a costume. The first **c** is pronounced as a **k: ak-•ses′•saw•ree.**
across	**ah•craws′** There is no *t* sound in this word.
acumen	**a•kyoo′•men.**
adult	Stress the second syllable, not the first: **a•dult′.**

aged When you use it as an adjective, pronounce both syllables: **an ā'•jed person.** When you use it as a verb, pronounce it as one syllable: **a person who ājd rapidly.**

á la mode "To the manner, to the way." Not limited to the ice cream on top of your pie. Say **ah•lah•mōd'.**

almond **ah'•muhnd.**

alumna Originally Latin (feminine form of **alumnus**). "A girl or woman who has attended or been graduated from a school or college." The plural form is **alumnae** (pronounced **ah•lum•nee'**).

alumnus From the Latin. "A boy or man who has attended or been graduated from a school or college." **Alumni (ah•lum•nī')** is the plural form.

amateur **am'•u•tur.** Not *am'•u•chur.*

ambassador **am•bas'•u•dur.** Not *am•bas'•u•dawr.*

anti- As in **antibiotic** and other words, it sounds better to say **an'•tee** than *an'•tī.*

apartheid **uh•part•hāt.** Say it as though it ended with a **t** instead of **d.** It refers to an official policy of racial segregation.

apricot **ap'•ri•caht.**

arctic **ahrk'•tic.** Pronounce that **c** in the middle.

aspirin **as'•pur•in.** There are three syllables to the word. Avoid the *aspern* and *asprin* pronunciations.

athletics **ath•le'•tiks.** This word has three syllables, never four.

auxiliary Pronounce **aug•zil'•ya•ree.** Make that four syllables.

baklava That Middle Eastern honey-and-nut pastry is **bah•klah•vah'.**

barbiturate Sound the second **r.**

basis Means "foundation." Remember that

	the plural form is **bases,** pronounced **bay′•seez.**
Beaujolais	Say **bō•zhō•lā′.** This is a red table wine.
berserk	**bur•surk′.** Sound both **r**'s.
bisect	**bī•sect′.**
boatswain	Pronounced **bo′•sun.** "A petty officer in charge of a ship."
borrow	Rhymes with **sorrow.** Avoid the *borry* pronunciation of the word.
bouillon	**boo′•yun.** "A clear broth or soup." Note BULLION.
bovine	Make the second syllable rhyme with **wine: bo′•vīn.** It means "like a cow."
brouhaha	**broo•hah′•hah.** "Hubbub, uproar."
bruit	**To bruit something about** is "to tell it; to let the word travel about." Pronounced **broot**—one syllable.
brut	"Dry, as champagne." Also **broot**— pronounce the **t.**
bullion	**bul′•yun.** "Gold or silver uncoined or in a mass.
cabinet	**kab′•in•et.** Three syllables.
calliope	**ka•lī′•ō•pee.** "A musical instrument whose pipes are sounded by steam pressure, used on riverboats and in circuses."
canapé	**kan′•u•pā.** "An appetizer."
caramel	**kair′•u•mel.**
Caucasian	**kaw•kā′•zhen.**
chafe	**chāf.** "To make sore by rubbing."
chaff	**chaf.** "The external envelopes, or husks, of grain."
chasm	**kaz′•um.** Sound that "k." A chasm is a yawning hollow, a deep gorge.
chassis	**shas′•ee.**
chic	**sheek,** not *chick* or *schick.*
chimney	**chim′•nee.** It has two syllables, not three, and an **n,** not an **i,** after the **m.**

chiropodist	ki•rah'•pe•dist. "One who treats foot ailments." Remember to pronounce the word as though it started with a **k**.
chocolate	All right to pronounce it as you did when a child—**chawk'•lit**.
coiffure	Pronounce it **kwah•fyoor'**.
colonel	**kur'•nul**.
comely	**kum'•lee**. "Of pleasing appearance." Does not rhyme with **homely**.
comptroller	A variant of the word **controller**. Used as the title for a financial officer. Pronounce it **kun•tro'•lur**.
conch	**kahnk** or **kanch**.
congratulate	**cun•gra'•tyoo•lāt**. Be sure to sound the **t** in the middle of the word.
connoisseur	**kahn•u•sur'**. "A competent judge of art or in matters of taste."
consummate	When you use the word as a verb, pronounce it **kahn'•su•māt**. When you use it as an adjective, meaning "extremely skilled," say **kahn'•soo•mit**.
creek	**kreek**. "A small stream of water, a brook." Do not confuse with **crick**.
crick	**krik** (rhymes with **sick**). "A muscle spasm."
cuisine	**kwi•zeen'**. "Style or quality of cooking."
culinary	**kyoo'•li•nair•ee**. "Of or pertaining to cooking or the kitchen."
dais	If you spell it correctly, you'll probably pronounce it correctly. It is **dā'•is**. The **a** has a long sound.
data, datum	**dāt'•ah; dāt'•um**. **Data** is the plural form of **datum**. Although **data** is widely used for both, it is comforting to know the difference.
deaf	**def**. Avoid the *deef* pronunciation.
debacle	**dā•bah'•kul**. "Sudden collapse; rout."

December	The word is not *Dezember*. Please do not sound a **z** in the pronunciation.
decrepit	It's a **t** on the end, not a **d**.
dentifrice	**den′•tu•fris.** Do not say *den′•tur•fris*.
despicable	**des•pik′•u•bul.** Means "contemptible."
desultory	**de′•zul•taw•ree.** "Random; now and then."
détente	"An agreement between nations to relax or ease aggression; its purpose is to reduce tension." Pronounce it **dā•tahnt′.**
detritus	**de•trī′•tus.** Loose particles or fragments.
diamond	**dī′•u•mund.** Let's hear all three syllables.
diaper	**dī′•u•pur.** It has three syllables.
dilettante	**dil•uh•tant′.** "One who dabbles in many things but masters none."
diphtheria	**dif•thir′•ee•u.** No *dip* sound in this word.
dirigible	**dur′•u•ju•bl.**
draught	Chiefly British. Pronunciation and meaning interchangeable with **draft.**
dreamed, dreamt	**dreemed; dremt.** Either of these words is correct.
ecstasy	**ek′•stah•see.**
ecumenism	**ek′•yoo•mēn′iz′um.**
elm	This word has one syllable; do not make it *el′•lum*.
ennui	**ahn•wee′.** Means "boredom, listlessness."
enroute	**ahn•root′.** "On or along the way."
entrée	**ahn′•trā′.** "The right to enter," or "the main course of a meal."
envelope	**en′•vah•lōp** if a noun; **en•vel′•up** if a verb.
environment	**en•vī•run•ment.** Let's hear that **n** in the middle.

epicurean	ep•i•kyoor•ee´•an.
err	ur.
escape	es•cāp´. There is no x in this word.
espresso	es•pres´•sō. Not *ex•pres´•sō*.
et cetera	et•set´•ur•u. Never say *ek•set´•ur•u*.
experiment	ek•sper´•u•ment. There is no *spear* in this word.
faux pas	"A blunder." Say fō•pah´, or else you will demonstrate what it is.
February	Feb´•roo•a•ree. Please pronounce both r's.
fiancé	fee•ahn´•sā. Pronounce this as you would the feminine word **fiancée**.
field	Be sure to sound the **d** at the end of the word.
fifth	There is an **f** in the middle.
film	The word has one syllable; do not say *fil´•um*. Or *flim*.
fiscal	fis´•kul. "Of or pertaining to finance." Do not confuse with *physical*.
fission	fizh´•un. Not fish´•in.
flaccid	flak´•sid. "Flabby."
flautist, flutist	flau´•tist is preferred. The first syllable rhymes with **now**.
forbade	The past tense of **forbid** is pronounced for•bad´.
forte	"That which one does most easily." It has one syllable (say **fawrt**); unless, of course, you're using the musical **forte** (meaning "loud"), and then you say **fawr´tā**.
foyer	fwah•yā´ was the original pronunciation, although most dictionaries accept foy´•ur.
fracas	fra´•kus. "A noisy quarrel."
gauche	gōsh. "Clumsy, tactless."

genealogy   **jee•nee•ahl′•u•jee.** Please note the **a** in the middle of the word.

genuine   **jen′•yoo•in.** Avoid making the last syllable rhyme with **vine.**

giant   Pronounced **jī′•ant,** not *jīnt.*

giblet   **jib•lut.**

government   **gu′•vurn•ment.** Be sure to sound the **n** in the middle.

granted   **gran•ted.** One should be able to take for granted that this word will not be confused with **granite.**

grievous   **gree′•vus.**

grocery   **grō′•sir•ee.** Make it three syllables.

guarantee   **gair•un•tee′.** The first syllable rhymes with **air.**

gynecology   You pronounce the **g** as you do in **girl.** It is **gī•nu•kahl′•u•jee.**

hallucinogen   **ha•loo′•si•ne•jen.** Confusing, because in **carcinogen** the accent is on the **sin.**

harass   **har′•us.** "To disturb or irritate." The accent is preferred on the first syllable.

harbinger   **hahr′•bin•jur.** Something that is a sign of what is to come.

height   **hīte.** Rhymes with **kite.**

help   Let's hear that **l.** The word is **help,** not *hep.*

herb   The preferred pronunciation is **urb.** Note that you do sound the **h** in **herbaceous** and **herbivore.**

homage   Let's hear the **h: hahm′•ij.**

homicide   Make sure you pronounce the first **i** as an **i** and not *o.* The word is not *homocide.*

hors d'oeuvre   **awr′•durv′.** Please note that you do not pronounce the **s.** [The French do not pronounce the final **s** when they use the plural form.] "An appetizer."

hosiery	**hō'•zher•ee.**
hospitable	The accent is on the first syllable.
huge	**hyooj.** Let's hear the **h** at the beginning of the word.
human	**hyoo'•mun.** Always pronounce the **h.** Do not say *yoo•mun.*
humble	**hum'•bul.** That **h** is sounded.
humor	Sound the **h: hyoo•mur.**
hundred	**hun'•dred.** The last syllable rhymes with **Fred.** Neither *hunnert* nor *hunderd* is correct.
hypnotize	This word has many mispronunciations. It is not *hit'•nu•tīze* or *hip'•mu•tīze.* Say **hip'•nu•tīz.**
idea	Say this aloud. Did you add an **r** to the word? It is not *idear.*
Illinois	**Il•u•noi'.** *Noise* in this word bothers many people.
indict	**in•dīt'.** Rhymes with **light.** It means "to charge (usually with a crime)."
integral	**in'•te•grul.** It means "essential to completeness." Make sure that the **r** is in the right place: Don't say *intregal.* It is not *in•teg'•ral,* either.
intermezzo	**in•tur•met'•sō.**
internecine	**in•tur•nes•ēn'.** Means "relating to a struggle within a group."
intravenous	**in•truh•vee'•nus.** Note that the word is not *in•ter'•ve•nous.*
irrevocable	**i •rev'•u•ku•bl.** "Irreversible."
Italian	**I•tal'•yun.** Do not say *Eye•tal'•yun.*
italics	**ĭ•tal'•iks,** not *ī•tal'•iks.* It means "cursive print," such as the type used to designate incorrect pronunciations in this section.
jabot	**zhah•bō'.** "A cascade of frills down the front of a shirt."

jamb   **jam.** Do not sound the **b.** Posts or pieces of a door or window frame.

jewelry   **joo'•el•ree.** It has three syllables.

jocose   **jō•kōs'.** "Joking."

jocund   **jawk'•und.** "Merry; of cheerful disposition."

jodhpurs   **jod'•purz,** not *jod'•furs.* The name derives from Jodhpur, a state of India.

junta   **hoon'•tah.** Give the **j** an **h** sound. It means "a group of military officers holding state power in a country after a *coup d'état.*"

just   Rhymes with **must.** Avoid the *jest* pronunciation.

juvenile   **joo'•vu•nul.** The last syllable does not rhyme with **mile.** It means "not yet adult."

karate   **ku•rah'•tee.** "A Japanese system of unarmed self-defense." The word literally means "empty-handed."

kibbutz   **ki•boŏts'.** The plural form is **kibbutzim: ki•boŏt•seem'.** A **kibbutz** is a "collective farm or settlement, usually in Israel."

kiln   **Kil** is still the preferred pronunciation.

kindergarten   **kin'•dur•gah r•tn.** It is not *kindergarden* or *kinny garden.*

kirsch   **kirsh.** Originally, "a colorless brandy made from the fermented juice of cherries."

knew   Pronounce **nyoo.**

knish   "Dough filled with meat or potato." Pronounce the **k.**

known   One syllable please: **nōn.**

lackadaisical   My favorite baseball manager is one of the many people who mispronounce this word. Pronounce it **lak•a•dā•zi•kul,** with no **s** in the second syllable.

lambaste	**lam•bāst'**. Slang. "To beat soundly, to scold severely."
larynx	**lar'•ingks**. It is not *lahr'•nicks*.
least	Pronounce the **t**.
length	**lengkth**. Avoid the *lenth* pronunciation.
liable	**lī'•u•bl**. Three syllables, in order not to confuse it with **libel**.
liaison	"A connecting link." It's pronounced **lee•ā'•zahn**, not *lee•u•zahn*.
library	**lī'•brair•ee**. Please pronounce the **r** in the middle.
long-lived	**lawng•līvd'** is preferable to *lawng•livd'*.
machinate	**mak'•i•nāt**. "To plot or to devise a plot."
maniacal	"Insane." Pronounce it **me•nī'•u•kul**.
manila	This term refers to a certain type of paper, usually buff colored. Don't mispronounce it as *vanilla* paper.
manufacture	**man•yoo•fak'•chur**. Be sure to sound the **u** in the middle of this word.
marinade	**mar•u•nād'**.
marshmallow	The chances are good that if you spell it correctly, you will also say it correctly. It is **marsh'•mal•lō**.
mayoralty	The accent is on the first syllable, just as it is in the word **mayor**.
melee	**mā'•lā**. "A confusing fracas."
memento	Pronounce the **e**'s, and never confuse this term with the word *momentous*.
menstruate	The word has three syllables: not *men'•strāte*.
mezzanine	**mez'•u•neen**.
milieu	**mē•lyoo'**. "Surroundings, environment."
miniature	**min'•ee•u•choor**. Please pronounce all four syllables. I still prefer the **t** sound for the last syllable, but most modern dictionaries give it the **ch** sound.

minutia	**mi•noo'•shee•u.** "A small or relatively unimportant detail." The plural of this word is **minutiae,** and you pronounce it **mi•noo'•shee•ee.**
mischievous	**mis'•chi•vus.** Three syllables only.
mnemonics	**ni•mahn'•iks.** This is a plural noun, but it is used with a singular verb. It means "a system to improve or develop the memory."
modern	**mahd'•urn.** Please do not say *modren.*
motor	**mō•tur.** That is a **t** in the middle.
mousse	**moos.** "A light dessert."
Muenster	**mŏŏn'•stur.** A creamy, fermented cheese.
NASA	**nas'•a.** National Aeronautics and Space Administration. Do not mispronounce this as *Nassau,* the city.
nomenclature	Enunciate the first two syllables; the word is not *normanclature.*
notary public	Not *notory republic.*
nuclear	**noo'•klee•ur.** The late president Eisenhower said *noo'•kyu•lur,* but of course no one outranked him, so his pronunciation went uncorrected.
offertory	The word has four syllables. Please note: There is no **a** in the middle of the word.
often	**off'•n.** The **t** is silent.
once	**wuhns.** This is a one-syllable word, without a **t.**
only	**ōn'•lee.** Do not say *olny.*
ophthalmologist	It means "eye doctor." It's **ahf•thal•mahl'•u•gist.**
orgy	**or'•jee.** It means "unrestrained indulgence."
panache	Say **pa•nash'.** It actually refers to a bunch of feathers or a plume. It also means "dash; verve."

particular	**pahr•tik′•yoo•lur.** Be sure to sound all four syllables.
patina	**pat′•u•nu.** "A shine or luster, or a coat of oxidation, as on brass or copper."
perfume	**pur′•fyoom** is preferred.
permanent	**pur′•mu•nent.** Do not reverse the **m** and the **n**.
persevere	Don't add an extra **r** before the **v**.
perspiration	**pur•spur•ā•shun.** The first syllable is **per**, not *pre*. A recent commercial presented a fashion designer who mispronounced this word.
petit	**pet′•ee.** Used in law. It means "minor" or "petty."
petite	**pu•teet′.** "Small, trim."
piano	**pee•an′•o.** Avoid the **pī•a•no** pronunciation. Also avoid changing the final **o** to an **a**.
picture	**pik′•chur.** Be sure to sound the **k** sound. *Pitch′•ur* is an unacceptable pronunciation for this word.
piquant	**pee′•kunt.** "Having an agreeably pungent or tart taste; provocative."
piquante	**pee•kahnt′.** Same meaning as above.
plagiarize	**plā•ju•rīze.** Use a **j** in the middle, not a **g** as in **girl**. "To use the ideas or writings of another as one's own."
poem	**po′•em.** Make that two syllables. No *pomes*, please.
poetry	**po′•e•tree.** Sound all three syllables.
poignant	**poin′•yent.** "Distressing; touching."
poinsettia	**poin•set′•ee•u.**
porcine	**pawr′•sīn.** "Like a pig."
posthumous	**pahs′•choo•mus.** "Occurring or continuing after death."
précis	**prā•see′.** "A summary." Don't be confused by the accent.

prelude The preferred pronunciation is **prel'•yood.**

proboscis **prō•bahs'•is.** A long snout, like an anteater's. Don't pronounce the **c.**

prohibition **prō•i•bi'•shun.** The **h** is silent.

protein You may say **pro'•teen** or **pro'•tee•in.**

proviso **prō•vī•zō.** "A limiting clause in a contract."

pumpkin . **pump'•kin.** Not *punkin.*

quasi **kwa'•zi.** "To some degree, almost, somewhat."

quay **kee.** "A wharf."

quiche **keesh.** "A custard, often with bacon and cheese, baked in an unsweetened pastry crust."

quiescent **kwē•es'•unt.** "Still; silent."

quiet **kwī•it.** This word has two syllables.

radiator **rā'•dee•ā•tur.**

rapport **ra•por'.** The **t** on the end of the word is silent.

ration You may say **rash'•un** or **rā'•shun.**

recognize The word is **rek'•ug•nīz.** Be sure the **g** in the middle is heard.

relapse Most people use **ree•laps'** for the verb and *ree'•laps* for the noun, but **ree•laps'** is correct for both.

relator The word you want is **Realtor.** Pronounce it **Ree'•ul•tr** and not *Ree•lā•tr.* Note that the **a** comes before the **l.** Refers to a real estate agent affiliated with the National Association of Real Estate Boards.

relevant **rel'•u•vent.** The **l** comes before the **v.**

remembrance **ree•mem'•bruns.** Three syllables. Please do not say *ree•mem'•ber•ans.*

reservoir **re'•zur•vwah.**

restaurant **res'•tawr•ahnt.** The word has three syllables, not two.

résumé	"A summing up." Pronounce it **re'• zoo•mā** or **rā'•zoo•mā**.
Revelation	The last book in the New Testament is **Revelation** (without an **s**).
revenue	**re'•ven•yoo,** not *re'•ven•oo*.
rinse	**rins.** Do not say *wrench* for **rinse**.
robust	It means "strong, healthy," and it's pronounced **ro•bust'**.
roof	Pronounce it **roof,** not *ruf*.
root beer	The **root** rhymes with **boot,** not *but*.
rosé	**rō•zā'.** "A wine that is suitable for either white or dark meat; it is pink in color."
route	Pronounce either **root** or **rowt**. The pronunciation **root** is given first in most dictionaries.
saboteur	**sab•u•ter'.**
sacrilegious	**sak•ru•lee'•jus.** "Irreverent."
sadism	**sā•diz'•um.**
sauterne	**sō•tairn'.** "A white table wine."
schism	**siz'•em.** "A separation."
scion	**si'•en.** "A descendant or heir."
sexual	**sek'•shoo•ul.** Not *seks'•yoo•ul*.
sherbet	**sher'•bit.** Note that it is not *sherbert*.
shown	**shōn.** One syllable.
similar	**sim'•i•ler.** "Resembling." Do not pronounce it *sim'•yoo•ler*.
sink	As it's spelled—not *zink*.
soiree	**swah•rā'.** "A party."
solder	**sahd'•r.** The **l** is silent.
soprano	Be sure to sound an **o** at the end of the word (it does not end with **a**.)
sotto voce	**sawt'•ō•vō•chee.** "Very softly; in an undertone."
species	**spee'•sheez.**
strength	**strengkth.** Do not say *strenth*.
suite	Pronounce it **sweet**. It means "a succession of related things: a series of con-

nected rooms; a matched set of furniture." Please note: you may have a **suit (soot)** of clothes, but you do not have a *suit* of furniture.

surprise   **sur•prīz'**. Note that the pronunciation is not *suh'•prīz*.

table d'hôte   **taw'•blu•dōt** (literally, "table of the host"). "Meal of the house served at a fixed price."

tarot   **ta•rō'**.

temperamental   This word has five syllables. Be sure to sound both the **er** and the **a** syllables in the middle of the word.

temperature   **tem'•pur•u•chur**. Pronounce all four syllables.

tenterhooks   Don't confuse this with *tenderhooks*, a nonword.

theater   **thee'•u•tur**. Do not say *thee•ā'•tur*.

thorough   **thur'•ō**. Never put an **l** in this word (making it *thorul*).

tired   **tīrd**.

toward   **Tord** is the preferred pronunciation in the United States.

tract   Do not say *tract* when you mean **track**.

Tuesday   It is **tyooz'•dā**, say the purists; **tooz'•dā** now appears in many dictionaries.

umbrella   **um•brel'•u**.

undoubtedly   **un•dau'•ted•lee**. Do not pronounce the **b** in **doubt**.

valet   **val'•et**.

vapid   **vap'•id**. "Tasteless, dull."

vaudeville   **vōd'•vil**.

vehement   **vee'•u•ment**. The **h** remains silent.

veldt   The word is sometimes spelled **veld**. It is pronounced **felt** or **veld**.

veterinarian   **vet•ur•u•nar'•ee•un**. There are six syllables. The word *vet* is not pleasing to most veterinarians.

via	Either **vī′•u** or **vee′•u.** is correct. (The meaning is usually restricted to "by way of"; "by means of" is not an accepted meaning.)
viaduct	**vī′•u•dukt.** Note that it is not *vī′•u•dahk.*
vice versa	You may say **vī′•see•vur′•su** or **vīs′• vur′•su.** I no longer laugh inwardly when I hear that first pronunciation. That's the way many experts say it.
vichyssoise	**vee′•shee•swahz.** Pronounce the final **s** as a **z.**
victuals	**vit′•ls.** "Food."
vignette	**vin•yet′.** "Ornamental design; a picture; a short literary composition."
virago	**vi•rā′•gō.** "A bad-tempered woman."
voyeur	**vwah•yur′.** A person who obtains gratification by looking at sexual objects or scenes.
wash	Please do not say *wawrsh.* There is no **r** in the word.
Washington	The first syllable does not have an **r** in it.
Westminster	No *minister* here, please.
whale	There is an **h** in the word. It is pronounced **hwāl,** and rhymes with **mail.**
what	**hwaht.** Sound the **h.**
when	**hwen.** Sound the **h.**
where	**hwair.** Sound the **h.** And the word rhymes with **care,** not *car.*
which	**hwich.** Sound the **h.**
while	**hwīl.** Sound the **h.**
white	**hwīt.** Sound the **h.**
with	Pronounce the **th** as you do in father.
wrestle	Not *ras′•sel,* but **res′•ul.**
Xavier	**Zā′•vee•ur.**
yellow	Avoid the *yella* pronunciation.
zoology	**zō•ahl′•u•jee.** The first syllable rhymes with **go** rather than with *to.*

4

BEYOND THE BASICS

For last year's words belong to last year's language
And next year's words await another voice.

—T. S. ELIOT
Little Gidding

The words I want to talk about in this section touch on the subtleties of language. Most are neither right nor wrong. But they do leave traces of where you've been and who you've been.

- They reveal the extent of your education—in some instances, the extent of your parents' educations.
- They tell whether you're young or old, contemporary or old-fashioned.
- They tell whether you're observant.
- They tell whether you've traveled.
- And they have a lot to do with where you're going and who you're going to be.

I credit Vance Packard's *The Status Seekers* with my idea for a collection of upscale and down-scale words. But I couldn't stop with just snob words. For the more I studied the effect of word choice, the more I realized that words describe the person using them.

There are new words, dated words, old words, young

words, rich words, and poor words. There are political words too—words that tag the speaker as liberal or conservative. An aura often hovers about a word—a connotation that you won't find explained in any dictionary. This aura influences the listener's response to the speaker.

I've worked on my list of upscale and down scale words for years. Perhaps you saw them in a chapter called "Help for 'hear'-ache" in *Martin's Magic Formula for Getting the Right Job*. In that book I called them "plus and minus words," because the reflection they cast on the speaker is shaped by more than mere station in life. Writing on this theme of words working *for* or *against* the speaker, I also referred to "plus and minus words" in articles I did for *Aloft* and *Writer's Digest* magazines. The chances are even greater that you saw William Safire's collection of such words in recent "On Language" columns in *The New York Times*.

I can tell you I was elated over a particular column; Safire called it "Caste Party." In it, he referred to *my* list—bless him—and then included some of my words with his.

I was even more elated when he gave me permission to use his words as well as his headings in this chapter. His headings are more to the mark than mine. He refers to "Out-of-it" words and "On-top-of-it" words. Following the principle that one should adopt apt words and phrases, I shall do just that. Here then, you have my latest and greatest collection of "Out-of-it" and "On-top-of-it" terms.

Do remember as you look at this list that I spend a lot of my life as a columnist; the reporting instinct is strong. I'm following it here. I am *reporting* on the listener's response to words. I am not responsible for that response.

OUT-OF-IT WORDS	ON-TOP-OF-IT WORDS
a hold of	**reach**
air corps (Use to refer to the old air corps only.)	**air force**

OUT-OF-IT WORDS   ON-TOP-OF-IT WORDS

OUT-OF-IT WORDS	ON-TOP-OF-IT WORDS
bathing suit	**swimsuit**
bathrobe (for a woman)	**hostess gown** or **robe**
bawl out	**scold, reprimand**
better half	**wife, husband**
blackboard	**chalkboard** (Black is no longer the prevailing color of chalkboards.)
bride and groom	**bride and bridegroom**
British citizen	**British subject**
bushes	**shrubs**
butcher	**meat cutter**
cake of soap	**bar of soap**
car wreck	**car accident**
chaise lounge	**chaise longue,** pronounced **shāz long** (If you learn to spell **longue,** you'll have no more trouble with this.)
chief justice of the Supreme Court	**chief justice of the United States**
Chinaman	**Chinese, someone from China**
claim	**say**
clap	**applaud**
cleaning woman	**domestic**
coffeepot	**coffee maker**
coffee table	**cocktail table**
colored, Negro	**Black, African-American**
costume jewelry	**fashion jewelry**
cuss	**curse**
deaf and dumb	**deaf, hearing impaired** (Most persons who have hearing impairments do speak.)
dig an oil well	**drill an oil well**
dishrag	**dishcloth**
dish towel	**tea towel**
drapes	**draperies**

OUT-OF-IT WORDS   ON-TOP-OF-IT WORDS

drugstore	**pharmacy**
eats	**food**
electric (as in *The electric is off.*)	**electricity** or **electric power**
ex-husband	**former husband**
fireman	**firefighter**
fish tank	**aquarium**
folks	**parents, family, relatives**
funnies	**comics**
gal or girl (for an adult female)	**woman**
galoshes	**boots, rubbers, overshoes**
girlfriend, boyfriend	**friend**
graduated	**was graduated from**
graveyard	**cemetery, memorial park**
grip	**bag, baggage, suitcase**
gym (in reference to health club)	**spa**
hair (One sometimes refers to hair and says, *shampoo them.*)	**hair**—Shampoo **it,** not *them,* is correct.
half-a-dollar	**fifty cents**
heavyset	**overweight**
hi-fi	**stereo**
home (as an edifice)	**house**
hopefully	**I hope**
icebox	**refrigerator**
idiot	**brain damaged**
lame	**disabled**
machine (for automobile)	**automobile, car**
maiden name	**birth name**
manpower	**human energy, human power**
material, goods	**fabric**

OUT-OF-IT WORDS	ON-TOP-OF-IT WORDS
middle age	**midlife**
the missus, the mister	**my wife** or **Mrs. Martin** or **Phyllis; my husband** or **Mr. Martin** or **Bruce**
movies	**films**
of a night	**at night**
out loud	**aloud**
passed away	**died**
piano player	**pianist**
picture (when you mean **painting**)	**painting**
pocketbook	**handbag**
porch	**deck**
postman	**mail carrier**
present	**gift**
press conference	**news conference** (Use **press conference** only if conference is limited to members of the press.)
Princess Diana	The word from Buckingham Palace is that she should be referred to as **The Princess of Wales.**
railroad station	**train station**
Reverend or Rev. Campbell	**the Rev. Mr.** (or **Dr.**) **Campbell**
rouge	**blusher**
row house	**town house**
Sahara Desert	**Sahara** (**Sahara** means "desert," so you don't need to repeat the word.)
sassy	**saucy**
shelves	**wall system** or **unit**
shot (as in medicine)	**injection**
Sierra Mountains	**Sierras** (*Mountains* is inherent in **Sierras,** of Spanish derivation, so you don't need to say *mountains* twice.)
Smithsonian Institute	**Smithsonian Institution**
sneakers	**running shoes**

OUT-OF-IT WORDS	ON-TOP-OF-IT WORDS
socket	**fixture**
soprano singer	**soprano** (It is all right to refer to a soprano saxophone.)
square	**block**
stewardess	**flight attendant**
stockings	**hose, hosiery**
subordinate	**staff**
switchboard	**console**
tease (as hair)	**back comb**
They got married.	**They were married.**
trunks	**shorts**
tux	**black tie**
undertaker	**funeral director**
unwed mother	**single mother**
vet	**veterinarian**, or **doctor of veterinary medicine**
washrag	**washcloth**
Wimpleton	**Wimbledon,** pronounced **wim′•b′l•dan** (if you are referring to the site of the famous tennis matches)
women's lib	**women's liberation**
yeah	**yes**

Want a few more hints on plus and minus words? Here's a column from Ann Landers that contains several new examples:

Phyllis Martin has a few words for Ann Landers

DEAR ANN LANDERS: Why all the fuss because a TV news commentator says, "Febyooary," when all around us we hear "cold slaw," "sherbert," "realator," and "irregardless"—to mention just a few nerve grinders? The abuse of the English language has become so commonplace that our ears will soon be accustomed to non-words and atrocious usage. Please do your bit by printing this, Ann. I'm signing myself—In Need Of Earmuffs.

DEAR EAR: Funny you should write today. I just read a book by Phyllis Martin, a Cincinnati job counselor and business consultant and a columnist for the Cincinnati Post. It's "Word Watcher's Handbook" (McKay, publisher, a paperback, $3.95). While the author didn't say anything about "cold slaw," "sherbert," or "realator," "irregardless" was listed right up with words that are obsolete.

Phyllis also tells us it is better to say "over" than "overly." She asks that we avoid "over with." Just plain "over" will do.

"Personal friend" is one word too many. "Friend" is enough. The same goes for "personal opinion." If it's your opinion, it's personal.

Anyone who says "needless to say" is saying too much. If it was needless, you wouldn't be saying it.

"Muchly" was O.K. a few hundred years ago but it's a bit much now.

Don't say "enthused" when you mean "enthusiastic."

The word is "famous," not "famed."

"Fantastic" is probably one of the most overworked words of our time. Get out of the rut and look up synonyms. You will be surprised to discover what the word fantastic really means.

"Gentlemen"—not "gent," please.

"Heartrendering" is not a word. It's "heartrending." Fat is rendered, not hearts.

"At this point in time" and "frame of reference" are children of Watergate and everybody is sick to death of them.

"Gross" is overused, especially by the young. Try "vulgar" or "coarse."

The phrase "I don't think" is another dud. How can you express an opinion if you don't think? Say instead, "I think not."

"Hisself" is not a word. "Himself" is what you are after.

"Learning experience" doesn't mean anything. Either you learn from experience or you don't.

Not all "h's" should be dropped, as in "honorable." Don't say "umble," say "humble."

"Unbeknownst" is a pompous substitute for the simple word "unknown." Don't be stuffy.

Phrases that grate from overuse are, "You can say that again"—"See what I mean"—"Due to the fact"—"How about that?" (You can also add to the list, "Have a nice day," and "Is it hot enough for you?")

Some of the most often mispronounced words are "knew"—it's not "noo," it's "nyoo." "Jewelry" is not "jool-ry." It's "jew-el-ree"—THREE syllables. "Prohibition" is "PRO-I-BI-SHUN." THE "h" is silent.

How many of you readers learned something today? I did. The book is fantastic—er —uh—I mean I'm enthused—pardon me—enthusiastic about it.

BRAND NAMES

Many manufacturers have lost their trademarks as a result of indiscriminate use of brand names. Limit your use of the following names to those times when you refer to the product or manufacturer in question.

Band-Aid	adhesive bandage
Clorox	bleach
Coca-Cola	cola
Coke (Coke is a registered name for Coca-Cola.)	cola
davenport (This word is now considered old-fashioned.)	sofa, divan
fax	telecopier
fiberglas	fiberglass
Formica*	laminated plastic
Frigidaire	refrigerator
IBM	computer
Jell-O	gelatin
Kleenex	facial tissue
Magic Marker	felt-tipped pen
plexiglas	acrylic plastic
Scotch tape	cellophane† tape or transparent tape
styrofoam	polystyrene plastic
TelePrompTer	prompting device

---

*The manufacturers of Formica almost lost exclusive rights to their famous trademark because people grew careless and referred to all laminated plastic as Formica. It took congressional action to save the word. See why manufacturers wince when you misuse their trademarks?
†The word cellophane was originally Cellophane, a trademark. The manufacturer lost exclusive rights to the word because people used it as a generic term.

thermos	vacuum bottle
Vaseline	petroleum jelly
Xerox	copier

AN AWARENESS TEST

This test is designed to remind us that it takes a lot of listening and looking if our lines of communication are going to be free of blockages.

Scoring: Give yourself ten points for each correct answer.

1. How would you refer to the bride of the Prince of Wales?
   a. Princess Diana
   b. The Princess of Wales

2. Which is preferred?
   a. *Oxfordians* are proud of their university.
   b. *Oxonians* are proud of their university.

3. Does this sentence sound all right to you: "We were pleased to hear that San Franciscans are riding trolley cars again"?

4. If I were quoting the poet Thomas Gray, would I say
   a. "all that glisters" is not gold, *or*
   b. "all that glistens" is not gold?

5. Is this an accurate quotation: "Money is the root of all evil"?

6. What is wrong with this sentence: "She is going to premiere in his play"?

7. What is wrong with this statement: "I second the nomination"?

8. Is a moderator correct in asking for a motion to adjourn?

9. Which is correct?
   a. chaise longue
   b. chaise lounge

10. I recently wrote to The Proctor & Gamble Company. Did I spell the name correctly?

11. What is the appropriate verbal offering to the bride and groom in a receiving line?
    a. best wishes to the bride and congratulations to the groom
    b. congratulations to both the bride and bridegroom

12. If train mishaps are called wrecks and planes crash, what term is used with the word *car*?
    a. crash
    b. accident

13. Which is the correct phrase?
    a. between you and I
    b. between you and me

14. Which is the proper phrasing?
    a. The church was built in the sixth century A.D.
    b. The church was built A.D. 570.
    c. The church was built in 570 A.D.

15. Subtract an automatic ten points if you fall back on the word *like* to express your thoughts and feelings. Does the following example sound like you?

You are describing a situation you handled on the phone with an angry customer and you say, "This person keeps yelling at me, and I'm like . . . [pause] what am I supposed to do? So I'm like frustrated."

Subtract another two points if you often say *he goes* instead of **he says.**

Key:

1. The word from Buckingham Palace is that she should be referred to as **The Princess of Wales.**

2. **Oxonian** is preferred.

3. As in the song, it's "little **cable** cars climb halfway to the stars."

4. The actual quotation:
   "Not all that tempts your wand'ring eyes
   And heedless hearts, is lawful prize;
   Nor all, that glis**ters**, gold."

   Yes, I was surprised too.
   Thanks for setting me straight, Jim Fallon.

5. The correct quotation—from the Bible—is:
   "The **love of** money is the root of all evil"—I Timothy 6:10.

6. The word *premiere* is not a verb. It is a noun.

7. It is not necessary for anyone to second a nomination. Furthermore, a moderator should not ask for a second to a nomination. Reason? It could cause embarrassment to the nominee if a second were not forthcoming.

8. No. When the business for which the meeting was called has been transacted, the moderator may declare the meeting adjourned.

9. It is **chaise longue,** pronounced **shāz long.**

10. No. **Procter** is spelled with *er* at the end. It is not Proct*or*.

11. It is proper etiquette to offer best wishes to the bride and congratulations to the bridegroom.

12. People in cars have accidents.

13. It's **between you and me.** Many readers begged for an entire section to be devoted to this point of grammar. Even Ann Landers mentioned it in one of her columns, saying, ". . . my hackles go up and I must fight with myself to keep from saying, 'Please! It's between you and ME.'"

14. **B** is the only correct phrasing. A.D., an abbreviation for the Latin term anno Domini, means, literally in the year of the Lord." Thus, responses **a** and **c** contain a redundancy and are incorrect.

Scoring

140	You rub everyone the right way. Congratulations.
120–130	You are very astute.
100–110	You are above average in awareness.
80–90	You need to grab your share of listening time.
0–70	You will need to increase the amount of reading you do, as well as the amount of listening.

Note: The truly observant reader will have noted the answers to numbers 1 and 9 in the word list on pages 80–84 and thereby raised the awareness score.

5

REVIEWING FOREIGN MENU TERMS

I am indebted to Marjabelle Young Stewart and Marian Faux for permitting me to include this segment on French menu terms for you. It was because I referred to Stewart's and Faux's book *Executive Etiquette* in a television "job spot" (for WKRC-TV, Cincinnati) that I learned that they and I have the same editor, Barbara Anderson.

I would like to show you more of the *Executive Etiquette* material but this is *my* book. Now that you know St. Martin's Press is the publisher, you can acquire your own copy of *Executive Etiquette*. You'll like Marjabelle Stewart's *The New Etiquette*, too.

I am also indebted to Librairie Larousse for permission to reprint the French pronunciation key from the *Larousse English-French:French-English Modern Dictionary*.

Familiarity with some foreign words and expressions is the mark of an educated person, to say nothing of the fact that it will help you to order food in a French or Italian restaurant, find the right train in Germany, and read some scholarly works. The most commonly used foreign words and phrases come from French, German, and Latin.

A word of warning here: Knowledge of foreign words and expressions should be put to discreet use. Sprinkling one's conversation with foreign words does not show that one is well traveled; it indicates that one is showing off. A parallel can perhaps be drawn between knowing and using foreign expressions and knowing how to play a bagpipe: A gentleman, it has been said, is someone who knows how to play the instrument but refrains from actually doing so.

The best way to feel secure in using foreign expressions is to hear someone else speak them, so don't be shy about asking an expert speaker in a language how to say something or taking a few language lessons. There are also many good books on foreign grammar and speaking that will help you become familiar with useful expressions.

FRENCH CUISINE

The foreign terms that Americans are most likely to encounter are those found on menus in French restaurants. Here is a list of the most commonly used expressions (a pronunciation key is on pages 100–101):

agneau [añô]	lamb
ail [ay]	garlic
à la [a] [la]	in the style of
amandine [amɑ́din]	made with almonds; often used in preparing fish fillets
artichauts [artiʃo]	artichokes
asperges [aspɛrʒ]	asparagus
aubergine [oberʒi:n]	eggplant
au jus [o] [ʒy]	in its own juice
au lait [lɛ]	with milk
avocat [avɔka]	avocado
baba au rhum [baba] [rɔm]	cake soaked in rum after it has been baked
banane [banan]	banana
basilic [bazilik]	basil
béarnaise [bearnez]	thick sauce made with shallots, tarragon, thyme, bay leaf, vinegar, white wine and egg yolks, served with grilled or sautéed meat or grilled fish

béchamel [beʃamɛ:l]	sauce of milk thickened with butter and flour
beurre d'ail [bœ:r] [a:j]	garlic butter
beurre noir [nwa:r]	brown butter served on eggs, fish, or vegetables
bière [bjɛ:r]	beer
biscuits [biskyi]	cookies
bisque [bisk]	soup, usually made of puréed shellfish
boeuf [boef]	beef
boeuf bourguignon [burgiɲɔ̃]	braised beef prepared in the style of Burgundy (with small glazed onions, mushrooms, and red wine)
boeuf rôti [roti]	roast beef
bombe glacée [bɔ̃:b] [glase]	ice-cream dessert
bonbon [bɔ̃]	candy
bordelaise [bɔrdəlɛz]	brown sauce made with wine and bone marrow
bouillabaisse [bujabɛs]	fish chowder on French Riviera; made with fish, olive oil, tomatoes, and saffron with water or bouillon
bouilli [bu ji]	boiled
braisée [brɛ ze]	braised
brioche [bri jɔʃ]	a kind of French bread
brochette [brɔ ʃɛt]	a skewer; anything cooked on a skewer may be called a brochette
brocoli [brɔkɔli]	broccoli
brouillé [bruje]	scrambled
café glacé [kafe glase]	ice cream with coffee flavoring
calmar [kal mar]	squid
canard [ka nar]	duck
caneton [kantɔ̃]	duckling
carottes [karɔt]	carrots
cassoulet [kasule]	stew made with white beans and pork
champignons [ʃɑ̃piɲɔ̃]	mushrooms

chateaubriand [ʃtobrijã]	cut of beef, grilled and served with vegetables cut in strips and with a béarnaise sauce
choix [ʃwa]	choice
choux de Bruxelles [ʃu] [brysɛl]	brussels sprouts
ciboulette [sibulɛt]	chives
citron [sitrɔ̃]	lemon
coeurs d'artichaut [kœr] [artiʃo]	artichoke hearts
consommé [kɔ̃sɔ̃me]	meat stock that has been enriched, concentrated, and clarified
coq au vin [kɔk] [o] [vɛ̃]	chicken in a red wine sauce with mushrooms, garlic, small onions, and diced pork
coquillages [kɔkijaʒ]	shellfish
coquilles Saint-Jacques [kɔki]	scallops
cornichon [kɔrniʃɔ̃]	type of small pickle, served with pâté and other dishes
côte de veau [vo]	veal chop
courgette [kurzet]	zucchini
crabe [kra:b]	crab
crème [krɛm]	custard or cream
crème brûlée [bryle]	a rich dessert pudding made with vanilla and cream; lightly coated with sugar, it is placed under the broiler, then cooled for two to three hours before serving
crème caramel [karamɛl]	custard with a burnt-sugar flavor
crème Chantilly [ʃɑ̃tji]	whipped cream
crêpes [krɛ:p]	thin pancakes
crêpes suzette	thin dessert pancakes topped with a sauce made with curaçao and the juice of mandarin oranges; usually served flaming
crevettes [krəvɛt]	shrimp

croissant [krwasɑ̃]	crescent-shaped roll made with a puff pastry or yeast dough; most often served at breakfast
croque-madame [krɔk]	chicken and cheese sandwich, grilled
croque-monsieur [məsjø]	ham and cheese sandwich, fried
croûtons [krutɔ̃]	bread that has been diced and sautéed in butter; used in soup and on salads
crudités [krydite]	raw vegetables served as an appetizer
demitasse [dəmitɑ:se]	strong, black coffee served in a small cup
en croûte [krut]	baked in a pastry crust
entrecôte [ɑ̃trəko:t]	translates as "between the ribs"; steak cut from between two ribs of beef, usually grilled or fried
épinards [epina:r]	spinach
escalopes de veau [ɛskalɔp]	thin, boneless slices of veal
escalopes de veau cordon bleu [kɔrdɔ̃ blø]	thin, boneless slices of veal with ham and cheese
escargots [ɛskargo]	snails
farci [farsi]	stuffed
filet mignon [miɲɔ̃]	small, choice cut of beef prepared by grilling or sautéeing
flambé [flɑ̃be]	describes a dish that has been ignited after being doused in a liqueur
florentine, à la [flɔrentin]	foods cooked in this style (usually eggs or fish) are put on spinach, covered with Mornay sauce, and sprinkled with cheese
foie gras [grɑ]	the livers of fattened geese and ducks
fraises [frɛ:z]	strawberries
framboises [frɑ̃bwa:z]	raspberries
frappé [frape]	chilled
frites [frit]	french fries

fromage [frəma:ʒ]	cheese
fruits de mer [fryi] [mɛr]	seafood
garni [garni]	garnished or decorated
gâteau [gɑto]	cake
gigot d'agneau [ʒigo] [aɲo]	leg of lamb
glace [glas]	ice cream
gratin, au [gratɛ]	prepared with a topping of toasted bread crumbs; usually includes grated cheese
haricots [ariko]	beans
hollandaise [ɔlɑ̃dɛ:z]	sauce made with egg yolks and butter; served over vegetables and fish
hors d'oeuvre [ɔ:r] [œ:vr]	appetizers, hot or cold
julienne [ʒyljɛn]	meat or vegetables cut into thin strips
lait [lɛ]	milk
laitue [lɛty]	lettuce
lapin [lapɛ̃]	rabbit
légumes [legym]	vegetables
lyonnaise [liɔ̃nez]	prepared with onions
madeleine [madlɛn]	sweet made from flour, butter, eggs, and sugar, baked in shell-like molds
madrilène [madrilɛn]	clear chicken soup with tomato; served chilled
maison [mɛzɔ̃]	a term applied only to recipes that are exclusive to the restaurant's owner or chef but usually used more loosely to mean in the style of the restaurant
maître d'hôtel [mɛ:tr] [otɛl]	headwaiter
médaillon [medajɔ̃]	food cut into a round or oval shape
menthe [mɑ̃:t]	mint
meunière [mønjɛ:r]	method of preparing fish; the fish is first seasoned, floured, and fried in butter, then served with lemon juice, parsley, and melted butter

Mornay [mɔrnɛ]	white sauce with cheese added
moules [mul]	mussels
mousse [mus]	a light, airy dish made with cream and eggs; may be of fish, chicken, fruits, or chocolate; served hot or cold
moutarde [mutard]	mustard
nature [naty:r]	plain; without trim; in its natural state
niçoise, à la [niswaz]	a dish cooked in the style of Nice, often prepared with tomatoes, zucchini, garlic, potatoes, green beans, olives, garlic capers, and anchovies
nouilles [nu:j]	noodles
oeuf [œf]	egg
oeufs bénédictine [benediktin]	in most American restaurants this refers to an egg and ham on an English muffin with hollandaise sauce and possibly a slice of truffle
oignon [ɔɲɔ̃]	onion
omelette [ɔmlɛt]	omelet; an egg dish
omelette aux fines herbes [fi:n]	omelet made with parsley, tarragon, and chives or another combination of herbs
pain [pɛ̃]	bread
papillote, en [papijɔt]	steamed, enclosed in a sheet of parchment
pâté [pɑte]	any dish of ground meat or fish baked in a mold that has been lined with strips of fat
pâté maison [mɛzɔ̃]	a pâté unique to a particular restaurant
pâtisseries [pɑtisri]	pastries
pêche [pɛ:ʃ]	peach
pêches melba	peaches that have been steeped in vanilla-flavored syrup, served over vanilla ice cream topped with raspberry purée

petit-beurre [pəti] [bœ:r]	butter cookie
petite marmite [pətit] [marmit]	clear soup made with meat, poultry, marrow bones, stockpot vegetables, and cabbage; usually served with toast and sprinkled with grated cheese
petit pain [pɛ̃]	roll
pilaf [pilaf]	rice sautéed in oil and cooked with a variety of seasonings
poisson [pwasɔ̃]	fish
poivre [pwa:vr]	pepper
pomme [pɔm]	apple
porc [pɔ:r]	pork
potage [pɔta:ʒ]	soup, usually with a cream base
pots de crème au chocolat [ʃɔkɔla]	rich chocolate dessert
poulet [pulɛ]	chicken
printanière, à la [prɛ̃tanje]	garnished with a variety of spring vegetables
prix fixe [pri] [fiks]	at a set price
Provençale, à la [prɔvãsal]	cooked in the style of Provence, usually with tomatoes, garlic, olives, and eggplant
purée [pyre]	food that has been mashed or put through a sieve or processed in a blender
quiche lorraine [kiʃ]	a tart made with eggs, cream, cheese, and bacon
ragout [ragu]	a dish made from meat, poultry, or fish that has been cut up and browned; may or may not include vegetables
ratatouille [ratatu:j]	a mixture of eggplant, zucchini, squash, onions, tomatoes, and peppers; may be served hot or cold
riz [ri]	rice
Robert [rober]	sauce of onion, white wine, and mustard; served with grilled pork dishes

saucisson [sosisɔ̃]	large sausage; sliced for serving
saumon [somɔ]	salmon
sec [sɛk]	dry
sel [sɛl]	salt
sorbet [sɔrbɛ]	sherbet; made from fruit or liqueurs
soufflé [sufle]	dish made with pureed ingredients, thickened with egg yolks and beaten egg whites; may be made with vegetables, fish, meat, fruit, nuts, or liqueurs; served as an appetizer, a main dish, or a dessert
spécialité de la maison [spesjalite] [mezɔ̃]	specialty of a particular restaurant
steak au poivre [pwa:vr]	steak made with crushed peppercorns
steak tartare [tarta:r]	uncooked ground meat seasoned with salt and pepper and served with a raw egg yolk on top and with capers, chopped onion, and parsley on the side
sucre [sykr]	sugar
sur commande [kɔmɑ̃d]	made to your special order
tarte [tart]	pie
thé [té]	tea
truffe [tryf]	truffle, a fungus that grows underground
truite [tryit]	trout
vichyssoise [viʃiswa:z]	a cream soup of leeks, potatoes, and chicken broth; served cold
vin [vɛ̃]	wine
vinaigrette [vinagrɛt]	sauce of oil, mustard, and vinegar, seasoned with salt and pepper and, at times, herbs
volaille [vɔla:j]	fowl, poultry

PRONUNCIATION KEY FOR FRENCH MENU TERMS

CONSONANTS

SYMBOLS	KEY WORDS
[b]	*bas* [bɑ]
[d]	*dame* [dam]
[dʒ]	*djinn* [dʒin], *bridge* [bridʒ]
[f]	*fin* [fɛ], *aphte* [aft]
[g]	*gris* [gri], *guerre* [gɛːr], *ghetto* [gɛto], *aggraver* [agrave], *second* [səgɔ̃]
[gn]	*gnome* [gnom]
[ɲ]	*pagne* [paɲ]
[gw]	*lingual* [lɛ̃gwal]
[gɥ]	*linguiste* [lɛ̃gɥist]
[gz]	*exempt* [egzɑ̃], *eczéma* [egzema]
[ʒ]	*jaspe* [ʒasp], *genêt* [ʒənɛ], *geai* [ʒɛ]
[°]	*héros* [°ero]
[k]	*caduc* [kadyk], *kaki* [kaki], *khédive* [keːdiːv], *écho* [eko], *ecchymose* [ɛkimoːz], *queue* [kø], *becqueter* [bɛkte]
[ks]	*équinoxe* [ekinɔks], *coccyx* [kɔksis]
[kw]	*quartz* [kwarts]
[l]	*lent* [lɑ̃], *bacille* [basil]
[m]	*mime* [mim], *gemme* [ʒɛm]
[n]	*nef* [nɛf], *bonne* [bɔn], *automne* [otɔn]
[p]	*part* [par], *appel* [apɛl]
[r]	*roi* [rwa], *terre* [tɛːr], *arrhes* [aːr]
[s]	*lis, lice* [lis], *ceci* [səsi], *scie* [si], *facétie* [fasesi], *garçon* [garsɔ̃]
[ʃ]	*chat* [ʃa], *schisme* [ʃism], *shampooing* [ʃɑ̃pwɛ]
[sk]	*scandale* [skɑ̃dal], *ski* [ski], *schizophrène* [skizofrɛn]
[skw]	*squame* [skwam]
[t]	*taupe* [toːp], *thé* [te], *sotte* [sɔt]
[tʃ]	*tchèque* [tʃɛk]
[v]	*vent* [vɑ̃], *wagon* [vagɔ̃]
[z]	*zèle* [zɛːl], *rose* [roːz]

VOWELS

SYMBOLS	KEY WORDS
[a]	*bague* [bag], *tabac* [taba], *surah* [syra], *drap* [dra], *plat* [pla], *orgeat* [orʒa], *femme* [fam]
[aː]	*tard* [taːr]
[ɑ]	*ras, raz* [rɑ], *bât* [bɑ]
[ɑː]	*sable* [sɑːbl], *âge* [ɑʒ]
[e]	*été* [ete], *pied* [pje], *bouchée* [buʃe], *crier* [krije], *volontiers* [vɔlɔ̃tje], *nez* [ne]
[ɛ]	*freiner* [frɛne], *legs* [lɛg], *sept* [sɛt], *abcès* [absɛ], *est* [ɛ], *archet* [arʃɛ], *reis* [rɛ], *bey* [bɛ], *vrai* [vrɛ], *laid, lait* [lɛ], *sagaie* [sagɛ], *rabais* [rabɛ], *faix* [fɛ]
[ɛː]	*treize* [trɛːz], *hêtre* [°ɛːtr], *paire* [pɛːr], *mère* [mɛːr]
[i]	*ni, nid* [ni], *lubie* [lybi], *fusil* [fyzi], *habit* [abi], *pris, prix* [pri], *riz* [ri], *jury* [ʒyri], *abbaye* [abɛi], *pays* [pei]
[iː]	*rire* [riːr], *abîme* [abiːm], *lyre* [liːr]
[o]	*franco* [frɑ̃ko], *accroc* [akro], *galop* [galo], *chaos* [kao], *sabot* [sabo], *au, eau, aulx* [o], *chaud, chaux* [ʃo], *haut* [°o]
[oː]	*aube* [oːb], *heaume* [°oːm], *rose* [roːz], *côte* [koːt]
[ɔ]	*tonne* [tɔn], *oignon* [ɔɲɔ̃]
[ɔː]	*éloge* [elɔːʒ], *mors* [mɔːr]
[ø]	*bleu* [blø], *queue* [kø], *nœud* [nø], *émeut* [emø], *œufs, eux* [ø]
[øː]	*veule* [vøːl], *jeûne* [ʒøːn]
[œ]	*seul* [sœl], *œuf* [œf], *cueillir* [kœjiːr]
[œː]	*peur* [pœːr], *œuvre* [œːvr]
[u]	*cou, coud, coût, coup* [ku], *boue, bout* [bu], *joug* [ʒu], *août* [u], *pouls* [pu], *goût* [gu], *houx* [°u], *remous* [rəmu], *saoul, sou, sous* [su]
[uː]	*rouge* [ruːʒ], *bourg* [buːr]
[y]	*cru, crû, crue* [kry], *rude* [ryd], *jus* [ʒy], *début* [deby], *flux* [fly], *ciguë* [sigy], *eu* [y]
[yː]	*ruse* [ryːz], *usure* [yzyːr], *bûche* [byːʃ], *gageure* [gaʒyːr]
[ə]	*le* [lə], *regard* [rəgaːr], *benêt* [bənɛ]

SEMI-VOWELS

SYMBOLS	KEY WORDS
[j]	*pieu* [pjø], *pléiade* [plejad], *joyeux* [ʒwajø], *grillon* [grijɔ̃], *maillon* [majɔ̃]
[w]	*wallon* [walɔ̃], *ouate* [wat], *quadruple* [kwadrypl], *jaguar* [ʒagwa:r] (cf. [kw], [gw])

CLUSTERS

SYMBOLS	KEY WORDS
[i:j]	*fille* [fi:j]
[œj]	*œillet* [œjɛ], *cueillette* [kœjɛt]
[œ:j]	*seuil* [sœ:j], *œil* [œ:j]
[øj]	*feuillet* [føjɛ]
[ø:j]	*feuille* [fø:j]

CLUSTERS
SEMI-VOWELS AND VOWELS

SYMBOLS	KEY WORDS
[wa]	*loi* [lwa], *froid* [frwa], *poids* [pwa], *proie* [prwa], *fois* [fwa], *doigt, doit* [dwa], *choix* [ʃwa], *ouate* [wat]
[wa:]	*loir* [lwa:r]
[ɥi]	*nuit* [nɥi], *muid* [mɥi], *pluie* [plɥi], *buis* [bɥi], *fruit* [frɥi], *puy* [pɥi]
[ɥe]	*arguer* [argɥe]
[a:j]	*bail* [ba:j], *cobaye* [kɔba:j], *maille* [ma:j]
[ɑ:j]	*bâiller* [bɑ:je]
[ɛj]	*grasseyer* [grasɛje], *balayer* [balɛje]
[ɛ:j]	*soleil* [sɔlɛ:j], *veille* [vɛ:j], *paye* [pɛ:j], *asseye* [asɛ:j]
[ij]	*pillage* [pija:ʒ]

NASALS

SYMBOLS	KEY WORDS
[ɑ̃]	*camper* [kɑ̃pe], *ancien* [ɑ̃sjɛ̃], *banc* [bɑ̃], *marchand* [marʃɑ̃], *sang* [sɑ̃], *céans* [seɑ̃], *paon* [pɑ̃], *tremblant* [trɑ̃blɑ̃], *fend* [fɑ̃], *encens* [ɑ̃sɑ̃], *tourment* [turmɑ̃], *empan* [ɑ̃pɑ̃], *temps* [tɑ̃], *exempt* [egzɑ̃]
[ɑ̃:]	*ange* [ɑ̃:ʒ], *ample* [ɑ̃:pl], *encre* [ɑ̃:kr], *semble* [sɑ̃:bl]
[ɛ̃]	*instinct* [ɛ̃stɛ̃], *vingt, vin, vain, vainc* [vɛ̃], *quint* [kɛ̃], *impie* [ɛ̃pi], *thym, tain* [tɛ̃], *saint, sein, seing, ceint* [sɛ̃], *essaim* [esɛ̃], *examen* [egzamɛ̃], *appendice* [apɛ̃dis], *viens* [vjɛ̃]
[ɛ̃:]	*linge* [lɛ̃:ʒ], *crainte* [krɛ̃:t], *geindre* [ʒɛ̃:dr]
[ɔ̃]	*non, nom* [nɔ̃], *plomb* [plɔ̃], *romps, rond* [rɔ̃], *prompt* [prɔ̃], *jonc* [ʒɔ̃], *bond* [bɔ̃], *long* [lɔ̃], *répons* [repɔ̃], *mont* [mɔ̃], *fonts* [fɔ̃], *lumbago* [lɔ̃bago]
[ɔ̃:]	*onde* [ɔ̃:d], *ombre* [ɔ̃:br], *jungle* [ʒɔ̃:gl]
[œ̃]	*alun* [alœ̃], *parfum* [parfœ̃], *jeun* [ʒœ̃], *emprunt* [ɑ̃prœ̃]
[œ̃:]	*défunte* [defœ̃:t], *humble* [œ̃:bl]

ITALIAN CUISINE

This segment is a result of reader requests. Italian cuisine is increasingly popular and this brief glossary will take you from **a** to **zuppa**. The following list includes the most common menu terms.

acqua [ak'kwa] — water

acqua minerale [ak'kwa mee ne rah'lay] — mineral water

agnello [an yel'loh] — lamb

anatra [ah'na tra]	duck
antipasto [ahn tee pa'stoh]	appetizer
aperitivo [a pe ree tee'voh]	aperitif
aragosta [a ra goh'sta]	lobster
arancia [ah rahn'cha]	orange
birra [bee rah]	beer
bistecca [bee stayk'ka]	steak
. . . .	*ben cotta* [ben kot'tah] well done
. . . .	*a mezza cottura* [ah me'dzah kot tu'rah] medium
. . . .	*al sangue* [ahl sahn'gwe] rare
burro [boor'roh]	butter
caffè [kaf fe']	coffee
. . . . .	*latte* [laht'te] coffee with milk
carne [kahr'nay]	meat
. . . . .	*di maiale* [dee ma yah'le] pork
. . . . .	*di manzo* [dee man dzoh] beef
cozza [kots'tsa]	mussel
fagiolini [fah jo li'ni]	string beans
fegato [fay'got toh]	liver
formaggio [for maj'joh]	cheese
fragole [frah'go le]	strawberries
frittata [freet tah'ta]	omelet
frutta [froot'ta]	fruit
frutti di mare [froot'tee dee mah're]	seafood
gamberetto [gam be rayt'toh]	prawn; shrimp
gelato [je lah'toh]	ice cream
granchio [gran'kyoh]	crab
insalata [een sa lah'ta]	salad
latte [lat'tay]	milk
lattuga [lat too'ga]	lettuce
legumi [le gu'mi]	vegetables

limone [lee moh ne]	lemon
maccheroni [mak ke roh'nee]	macaroni—tubular pasta
mela [me'lah]	apple
mellone [mil lo'ne]	melon
merluzzo [mayr loots'tsoh]	cod
minestrone [mee ne stroh'nay]	minestrone, a thick vegetable soup
mostarda [mo stahr'da]	mustard
olio d'olivia [o lyoh do lee'va]	olive oil
ostricas [o stree kas]	oysters
pane [pah ne]	bread
pasta [pa'sta]	pastry, pasta, dough. Pasta is the generic name for a wide range of noodles and noodle-related dishes. You'll recognize cannelloni, *maccheroni,* ravioli, and spaghetti; however, there are many more, and they come in a bewildering variety of sizes and shapes, such as tubes, ribbons, shells, strings, and stars.
patata [pa tah'ta]	potato
pesca [pay'ska]	peach
pesce [pay'she]	fish
pettine [pet'tee ne]	scallop
pollame [pol lah'me]	poultry
pollo [pohl'loh]	chicken
pomodoro [poa mo daw' roa]	tomato
prosciutto [pro shoot'toh]	ham
ravioli [ra'vee o lee]	ravioli, stuffed pasta casings
riso [ree'soh]	rice
rotolos [ro'to lohs]	rolls

sale [sah'le]	salt
salmone [sal moh'ne]	salmon
salsiccias [sal seech'chas]	sausages
tacchino [tak kee'noh]	turkey
uovo [wo'voh]	egg
vino [vee'noh]	wine
vitello [vee tel'loh]	veal. You probably know this word. If not, learn it. There's no way you can dine out in Italy without encountering veal on the menu.
vongole [von'goal lay]	clams
zucchero [tsook'ke roh]	sugar
zuppa [tsoop'pa]	soup

6

ENGLISH AS A SECOND LANGUAGE FOR AMERICANS

Reprinted by permission of Tribune Media Services.

We Americans have often been accused of being un-cultured because most of us know only one language. Many of our British friends say we don't even know that one. We do. It's just not the same one they know.

If you'd like to appear more cultured, to learn a second language, I offer an easy one for you. It's *English* English.

Take a look at my collection of American versus *English* English words. They'll help to remove a language barrier if you have occasion to talk with Britons or if you visit the United Kingdom. Then afterward, do a favour—whoops,

that's favor—for me, please, and send along your additions
to my glossary.

AMERICAN ENGLISH	ENGLISH ENGLISH
advertisement	advert
apartment	flat
artificial flowers	artificial flowers/everlasting flowers
baby carriage	pram
baby's diaper	nappy/napkin
baked potatoes	potatoes in their skins/jackets (Those Britons are formal about everything.)
ballpoint pen	Biro
Band-Aid	sticking plaster
biscuit	scone
block	block does not refer to street length but to a building, and the **next block** is the adjacent building
brights (lights on a car)	main beams
broil	grill
burglarize	burgle
busy signal	engaged
call me (on the telephone)	ring me
can	tin
candy	sweets
carry out	take away
clippings	cuttings
cookbook	cookery book
corn	maize
divided highway	dual carriageway (And, while we're on the **dual carriageway,** we talk about **overtaking cars**—passing cars is an Americanism.)

eggplant	aubergine
elevator	lift
the facilities	the loo/the WC
faucet	tap
fender	wing/mudguard
field hockey	hockey
flashlight	torch
flat	puncture (Stay with me; an apartment is a **flat.**)
football	rugby football (**Football** is also called **American football.**)
freeway	motorway
french fries	chips
garage sale	jumble sale
garters (See SUSPENDERS under American English.)	suspenders
gasoline	petrol
general information	gen
grocery cart	trolley
ham	gammon
hamburger	mince
hockey	ice hockey
hood of a car	bonnet
horn	hooter
hose	tights /stockings
hospitalized	in hospital
installment plan	the never-never (As **I'm buying it on the never-never.**)
license plate	number plate
line (get in line)	queue (get in the queue)
liquor store	off license/off premises
Main street	High street
makeup (or toilet) **kit**	sponge bag
mechanical pencil	propelling pencil
muffler (on a car)	silencer
nail polish	nail varnish

napkin	serviette (The word napkin is rather widely used now, but if you cause raised eyebrows when you say napkin, say **serviette**—quickly.)
newcomer	newcomer/incomer
nurse (baby)	nanny
nurse (hospital)	sister/nursing sister
packages	parcels
pants	trousers
parking garage, parking lot	car park
pavement (meaning the roadway)	road
peanuts	monkey nuts
potato chips	crisps
private school	public school
public school	state school
railroad	railway
raincoat	mackintosh/oilskin
Realtor	estate agent
rest stop	lay by
roast (leg of lamb, et al)	joint
rubber boots	Wellingtons, Wellies
run (as in pantyhose)	ladder
rutabaga	Swede
Santa Claus	Father Christmas
sausages	bangers
sedan	saloon
sneakers	trainers/plimsolls
soap flakes (or **detergent**)	washing powder
soccer	football (It may also be called soccer.)
sports (as a collective noun)	sport
squash	vegetable marrow
station wagon	estate car
stove	cooker

subway	underground
surplus labor	redundancies
suspenders	braces
sweater	jumper
tacky, unpleasant	grotty
television	tellie
telev ision commercial	tellie advert
traffic circle	roundabout (Go around to the left.)
trailer	caravan
trouser cuffs	turn ups
truck	lorry
trunk (of a car)	boot
underpants	pants
underthings (women's)	smalls (As in **I'm wearing my smalls.**)
vacation	holiday
washcloth	face flannel
wheat	corn
whistle (of factory)	hooter
windshield	windscreen
wrench	spanner
wrinkle free	uncrushable

I didn't include a favorite of mine in the glossary because it's such an oldie; after all, I've been collecting these Briticisms for years. But doesn't **penny dreadful** delight you, too? **Penny dreadful** refers to a pulp magazine.

Nor did I include the phrase **knock up.** However, I will remind you that when a Briton says **I'll knock you up,** you can expect nothing more than a knock at the door. Often the same word or phrase is used in the United States and the United Kingdom, but that word or phrase has different meanings. In this country if you say **roll-on** you're probably referring to a deodorant, while in Britain a **roll-on** is a girdle. And let's not forget that what Britons call the **first floor** we call the **second floor.** Our **first floor** is their **ground floor.**

There's no point in pretending that the words I show you here hold for every corner of the United Kingdom. We Americans are not always consistent either. **Going to the shore** sounds appropriate when I'm in New Jersey, but when I'm in California, I find myself headed **for the beach.** And, my **schedule** (pronounced **shed•yule** in Britain) didn't allow for a study of the many differences in pronunciation. But I will alert you to a few of the differences in spelling. For example:

AMERICAN SPELLING	ENGLISH SPELLING
airplane	aeroplane
center	centre
color	colour
curb (by pavement)	kerb (But I would **curb** my tongue.)
favor	favour
fervor	fervour
hodgepodge	hotch potch
jail	gaol
pajamas	pyjamas
tire	tyre
utilize	utilise

BRITISH PLACE NAMES

No doubt place names could inspire another chapter, maybe even a book, but cast your eyes on some of these and let them serve as a reminder to learn the proper term when possible. You might say **a person from** _____ if you're unsure of the proper word. I assure you that's what I did when I visited Little Piddle.

PLACE	PERSON
Birmingham	Brummie (slightly slangy)
Bristol	Bristolian
Cambridge	Cantabrigian
Harrow	Harrovian
Lancashire	Lancastrian
Liverpool	Liverpudlian
London	Londoner
Manchester	Mancunian
Oxford	Oxonian
Shropshire	Salopian

Should you visit Scotland, do remember that you refer to persons there as Scots. You drink Scotch, at least I do. Oh, yes, and a person from Glasgow is a Glaswegian.

Even with this handy glossary in hand, you'll want to have a British friend monitor your speech as you introduce new words into your vocabulary. If you're a writer who intends to write about England, your need for a British friend or editor is critical. You'll want to guard against referring to this friend as a British citizen. Say British subject. Great Britain is a monarchy.

7

TRAVELER'S ADVISORY: WELCOME WORDS

Now that everyone is traveling all over, it's time to consider whether the words we use when we get there add to our welcome.

You probably have a good command of the language. But do you make a point of finding out what you need to know about place names and the way certain words are used in different locales?

A QUICK QUIZ TO TEST YOUR TRAVEL SAVVY

To see how word wise you are, and to add to your wealth of words, take the following test:

1. Suppose I visit Hawaii and want to return home (home being one of the first forty-nine states). Do I say?
   a. I want to return *stateside*.
   b. I want to return to the *mainland*.

2. When visiting Mexico, is it better to tell my hosts?
   a. I am an American.
   b. I am a North American.

3. When I am in Washington, D.C., and I visit the famous museum, do I say
   a. The Smithsonian Institution, *or*
   b. The Smithsonian Institute?

4. If I visit the site of the famous tennis matches in England, do I say
   a. Wimbledon, *or*
   b. Wimpleton.

5. If I wish to please the royal family, do I refer to Diana as
   a. Diana, the Princess of Wales, *or*
   b. Princess Diana?

6. When I visit San Francisco, and I ride on those little cars that "climb halfway to the stars," do I refer to them as
   a. trolley cars, *or*
   b. cable cars?

7. When I visit Chicago, do I refer to Illinois as
   a. Ill•ih•noise, *or*
   b. Ill•ih•noy?

8. While still in Illinois, I visit Des Plaines. Do I say
   a. Des Plaines, *or*
   b. De Plain?

9. When I visit Jefferson's home in Virginia, do I pronounce Monticello as
   a. Mont•teh•chello, *or*
   b. Mont•teh•sello?

10. When in Italy, do I say?
    a. Eye•talian.
    b. It•talian.

11. When in Great Britain, do I refer to those who live there as
    a. British citizens, *or*
    b. British subjects?

12. When visiting Texas, do I talk about
    a. digging an oil well, *or*
    b. drilling for oil?

13. When visiting the state of Washington, do I pronounce Spokane as,
    a. Spō•can' *or*
    b. Spō•cane?

14. When visiting our western states, do I remark on the beauty of
    a. the Sierras, *or*
    b. the Sierra Mountains?

15. Do I refer to the climate in Arizona as
    a. healthy, *or*
    b. healthful.

16. Is the Netherlands a part of Holland?
    a. Yes
    b. No

17. If I visit Boston, do I refer to
    a. the Boston Common, *or*
    b. the Boston Commons?

18. When I'm in Louisiana, do I say
    a. New Órleans, *or*
    b. New Orleáns?

19. In New York City do I pronounce the Houston in Houston Street the same way I do when I'm in Texas?
    a. Yes
    b. No

20. If I am a graduate of a well-known New York university, is it
    a. Colombia, *or*
    b. Columbia?

21. Is Russia a part of the Soviet Union?
    a. Yes
    b. No

22. In Washington, D.C., it's Pennsylvania Avenue; in Indianapolis, is it
    a. Pennsylvania Avenue, *or*
    b. Pennsylvania Street?

23. You cruise aboard a
    a. ship, *or* a
    b. boat?

24. The correct term for someone who lives in the Canadian city of Quebec is
    a. Quebecois, *or*
    b. Quebekian?

25. What is the name of the famous Disney theme park in California?
    a. Walt Disney World
    b. Disneyland?

Answers

1. b. Hawaii is a state. Hawaiians do not appreciate your excluding them from statehood as you do when you say *stateside*. Say **mainland** instead.

2. b. Mexicans consider themselves Americans because Mexico is part of the Americas. You'll notice they refer to U.S. citizens as **norteamericanos.**

3. a. It's the **Smithsonian Institution.**

4. a. It's **Wimbledon.** If you'll remember to think of Wimble Downs, you'll pronounce it correctly. Sportscasters take note.

5. a. She's the **Princess of Wales.**

6. b. They are **cable cars.**

7. b. Try to remember that while Chicago may be noisy, when you say **Illinois,** no noise should be heard.

8. a. Sound the s in **Des** and in **Plaines.**

9. a. You'll remember this one if you'll picture Jefferson playing the cello (pronounced **chello,** of course).

10. b. **It•talian** is preferred.

11. b. If you'll remember that Great Britain is a monarchy, you'll remember that those who live there are **subjects.**

12. b. Texans will remind you that you might **dig holes,** but you **drill for oil.**

13. a. It is **Spō•can'**.

14. a. Say **Sierras** rather than the *Sierra Mountains*. Sierra, of Spanish derivation, inherently means "mountain," so you don't need to say this twice.

15. b. **Healthful** means "health-giving"; *healthy* means "possessing health."

16. b. It's the other way around. The **Netherlands** is a small kingdom lying on the North Sea in northwestern Europe. The country is often called **Holland;** however, Holland is the name of the two main western provinces.

17. a. It is the **Boston Common.**

18. a. **New Órleans** is the preferred pronunciation.

19. b. No. In New York City, it's **Houston (How•ston)** Street; in Texas, it's Houston *(Hew•ston)*.

20. b. It's **Columbia University.** *Colombia* is a country in South America.

21. a. The Soviet Union is composed of several republics, of which **Russia** is one.

22. b. **Pennsylvania Street** is correct.

23. a. An ocean liner is a **ship,** despite the familiar *Love Boat.*

24. a. **Quebecois,** pronounced **kā•bə'•kwä'**. Say **Quebecois (kā•bə•kwäz')** when referring to more than one person.

25. b. **Disneyland** is located in California; Walt Disney World is located in Orlando, Florida.

Scoring

If you missed fewer than five items, you are a very knowledgeable traveler and welcome wherever you go. If you missed six to eight items, you will want to be become attuned to new words and new situations. If you missed more than eight questions, your misuse of words is holding you back. You'll want to embark on a word-study mission in order to enhance your image.

8

OCCUPATIONAL HAZARDS OF THE VERBAL VARIETY

"First and foremost, the word is not '*nucular*.'"

© 1989 by Sidney Harris—*American Scientist* magazine.

Because I usually write about the most abused and misused words, I've not said a lot about words that annoy only a special segment of listeners. However, when the misuse of certain words can cost jobs, promotions, or at least credibility, it's time to sound an alert.

While most of us handle the words appropriate to our field of work quite well, we sometimes stumble when we're in unfamiliar territory. We fail to realize that just as we wince when "outsiders" mangle words that form a part of our occupational vocabularies, *they* wince when we mangle their words.

The words I highlight here made their way into this book because somebody—make that a great many somebodies—nominated the words for inclusion. No, this is not a complete list. It represents a most-often-complained-about selection. Please examine each entry very c-a-r-e-f-u-l-l-y to be sure you use the word or phrase correctly.

Those in the **airline industry** conclude we're not with it when we refer to a **flight attendant** as a *stewardess*. And, for job candidates in this field, I report this incident. A reader of my career column asked me to find out why a major airline failed to make an offer after three interviews at company headquarters. I was told that while the young woman made a positive first impression, she didn't seem as astute as they had hoped. She assured them she didn't get *air sick* and that she could have her little *train case* ready anytime. "My dear," my informant said, "we don't get air sick." If someone has an upset, it's **motion sickness.** Furthermore, the candidate said *stewardess* instead of **flight attendant,** and she looked blank when they used the word **carrier.** "No, of course we wouldn't have explained all this to her," the informant said, "and we ask that you don't."

This reminder from **bankers:** "We rent **safe-deposit boxes,** not *safety deposit boxes.*"

A frequent comment from **business** is this: "It's **fiscal year,** not *physical year.*" Also, the *personnel department* is now the **human-resources department.** A **console** has probably replaced the *switchboard.* And, *manna-facture* as a pronunciation instead of **manufacture** still grates on many ears.

A **butcher** usually works in a slaughterhouse. Your **meat cutter** serves you at the meat market.

Ceramists ask us again to pronounce **kiln** as though it were **kill.**

Those in the **construction industry** remind us that we may **cement** a walk—or even a relationship—but we pour **concrete**, not cement.

Please remember that **dentists** are doctors. They are offended when we say *dentists and doctors.* How about **dentists and physicians** instead?

Dog catchers are not around anymore. We now have **animal-control officers.**

Druggists are **pharmacists,** and my informal survey indicates that they prefer to be called pharmacists. "Unless," as one said, "you put friendly and neighborhood in front of the word **druggist.**"

Educators provide these reminders: The word **kindergarten** is pronounced as it's spelled—**kin•der•gar•ten.** It is not *kin•der•garden;* nor, heaven forbid, *kinnygarden.* One doesn't have to be a graduate to learn the following: **alumnus** (uh•lúm•nus) is the masculine singular form; **alumni** (uh•lúm•ni) is the masculine plural form. It is also used to refer to a group of men and women. **Alumna** (uh•lúm•nuh) is the feminine singular form; **alumnae** (uh•lúm•nee) is the feminine plural form. Also, the school **principal** likes you to spell the word with **pal** on the end.

I promised one educator I'd include educators' complaints if they'd promise to stop using overblown phrases— such as *motorized attendance module* for **bus.**

Your *fireman* is now your **firefighter.**

Food-industry representatives remind us that it's now **servers** instead of *waiters* and *waitresses.* Frequently mentioned word irritants include *cold slaw* for **cole slaw** and the mispronunciation of **cuisine** and **culinary.** Say **kwi•zeén** and **kyoó•lə•narē.** If you're a part of the industry or work with those in the field, you'll want to make a more exhaustive study of related words. Also note pages 91–104 in this book.

Hairstylists bristle at being called *beauticians*. Teasing and ratting are out and have been for a long time; if you must refer to the process, say **back combing.** Another reminder: You don't *wash* your hair, you **shampoo** it.

Those in **interior design** are not *decorators*. They tell me they also cringe at hearing the word **picture** pronounced *pitcher*. Say **pik'•chər.** Give the word a **k** sound in the middle. And, if you wish to buy a painting, say **painting;** do not refer to it as a picture. Wallpaper is now **wall covering,** and **window treatment** is the catchall phrase for what you use to cover windows: blinds, curtains, or draperies. One may drape windows, but those window coverings are draperies.

Those in **media** caution that **media** is a plural form of **medium.** You'll also want to note that while those in *print* media seem happy with *press* conferences, some of the snootier members of radio and television staffs prefer **news** conferences.

Those in the **medical** profession, or those who aspire to the profession, need a good, unabridged medical dictionary. This meager list merely demonstrates how entertaining some of our mistakes must be to those who know better. Examples: **Prostate** is a gland. *Prostrate* means prone. It is **larynx** (lar'•ingks), not *lahr'•nicks*. **Health care** is two words. Everyone has a **temperature;** sometimes it's high, sometimes it's low. The same holds true for **blood pressure.** We get **injections** (ouch) rather than shots. We say **persons with disabilities** rather than *handicapped persons*. It's our **rotator cuff** rather than *rotary cuff*. **Ophthalmologists** remind us that the **ph** in the first syllable of the word gets the **f** sound. **CDC** stands for **Centers for Disease Control** (Be sure to put the **s** on **Centers.**). Likewise, it's **The National Institutes of Health** and not *The National Institute of Health,* and it's **The Johns Hopkins University,** not *John Hopkins*. All of this serves as a warning to ask someone in the medical field about a medical term that puzzles. Make that two persons, and if they don't agree, ask a third.

While we used to go to the *movies,* we now see **films.**
The *policeman* is now called **officer.**

The *postman* is a **mail carrier.** Do remember that the card you request at the post office is a postal card; the ones with pretty pictures are postcards.

The **power-and-light** folks beg us to remember that *electric* is an adjective. We don't impress when we say *the electric is off.* Say **electricity** or **electric power.**

Realtors are tired of hearing an extra *la* in the middle of the name of their profession. We can pronounce this correctly by reminding ourselves that real estate deals with **real** property, not *reala* property. We make friends of **Realtors** if we also remember that the word is **capitalized.**

Those who make **religion** a profession often tell me they're tired of hearing **offertory** pronounced as though it had five syllables. It is not *of•fer•uh•to•ry;* skip the *uh.* Several ministers have asked that until members of the congregation learn that the last book of the Bible is the book of **Revelation** (not *Revelations*), they should refrain from passing critical notes about grammar to their minister.

Scientists conduct **experiments,** not *ex•spear•a•ments.* Also, they remind all of us again that the word is **nuclear,** not *nu•cu•lar.*

Speakers insist that they stand upon a **podium** (the word has the same base as **podiatry**) and place their notes upon a **lectern.** The **dais**—pronounced **day'•us**—is a raised platform.

Undertakers and *morticians* often prefer to be called **funeral directors.** And, we bury our loved ones in a **memorial park** or **cemetery** rather than in a *graveyard.*

My editor, Barbara Anderson, has given me the inside story on the things that annoy **editors.** She cast herself in the reader role and responded to my request for contributions to this edition. What's more, she sent a memo to her colleagues soliciting entries. "I'm getting memos with every delivery of mail!" she told me. It seems we've touched a nerve. Because everyone has a book inside him or her, it behooves each of us to take note on the latest from the **publishing world:**

Reporter Typographics, Inc., gives this test to prospective editors. And I thank them for permitting me to show it to you.

which word is rite? right?

surprise or suprise
dominant or dominent
receive or recieve
predictible or predictable
commemorate or commemmorate
extraordinary or extrordinary
occassional or occasional
separate or seperate
accomodate or accommodate
insistent or insistant
wierd or weird
incidently or incidentally
occurrence or occurrance
embarrassment or embarrasment
analogy or analagy
concientious or conscientious
optomism or optimism

surprise, dominant, receive, predictable,
commemorate, extraordinary, occasional,
separate, accommodate, insistent, weird,
incidentally, occurrence, embarrassment,
analogy, conscientious, optimism

R E P O R T E R

- Authors should be aware that their books contain **forewords,** not *forwards;* **afterwords,** not *afterwards;* **acknowledgments,** not *acknowledgements;* **prologues** and **epilogues,** not *prologs* and *epilogs.*
- Avoid using *this* as a noun when it's unclear what it's referring to. *This* flaw is especially bothersome when *this* appears at the start of a paragraph.
- Brush up on all uses of the verbs **to lie** (assume a horizontal position) and **to lay** (to place something somewhere). The most otherwise-literate authors never seem to get this right. See page 44.

- Writers of science fiction make a bad blunder when they refer to their genre as *sci-fi.* This term is generally out within the **SF** (or **science fiction**) community.
- A travel writer should know how to spell **accommodations**—with two **m**'s. Also that it's **Antarctica,** not *Antartica.*
- Any writer and any person working in publishing should know that the name of the industry's trade magazine is **Publishers Weekly,** not *Publisher's Weekly.*
- If you're trying to convince an editor that you're a seasoned free-lance writer, make sure you say that you've **written,** not *authored,* numerous articles and books. **Author** is always a noun, never a verb.
- Misspellings annoy all editors (especially if you are claiming to be an expert in a particular area) and kill opportunities for those seeking jobs in the editorial field.

Here are 110 additional words that can spell D.I.S.A.S.T.E.R. if misspelled. Authors, especially, take note!

The 110 Most Threatening Spelling Words

1. accept
2. accommodate
3. acknowledgment
4. acquaintance
5. across
6. affect
7. all right
8. a lot (*two* words)
9. already
10. among
11. analysis
12. apparent
13. appearance
14. arrangement
15. attendance
16. beginning
17. benefited
18. business
19. calendar
20. canceled
21. coming
22. commitment
23. committee
24. confident
25. conscientious
26. controversy
27. convenience
28. convenient

29. criticism
30. description
31. difference
32. dilapidated
33. dilemma
34. disappoint
35. effect
36. eligible
37. embarrass
38. endeavor
39. equipped
40. especially
41. exceed
42. except
43. existence
44. experience
45. explanation
46. extension
47. February
48. foreign
49. fourth
50. government
51. guarantee
52. height
53. immediately
54. incidentally
55. its
56. judgment
57. laboratory
58. liaison
59. loose
60. memento
61. minuscule
62. necessary
63. oblige
64. occasion
65. occurred
66. omission
67. omitted
68. opportunity
69. original
70. paid
71. pamphlet
72. personal
73. personnel
74. possession
75. practical
76. practically
77. preferred
78. principal
79. principle
80. privilege
81. probably
82. procedure
83. proceed
84. professor
85. quantity
86. questionnaire
87. really
88. receive
89. recommend
90. reference
91. referred
92. referring
93. sacrilegious
94. schedule
95. separate
96. similar
97. sincerely
98. stationery
99. strictly
100. their
101. there
102. too
103. undoubtedly
104. unnecessary
105. using
106. volume
107. weather
108. Wednesday
109. whether
110. writing

9

CLEARING A PATH IN THE WOODS

A Word fitly spoken is like apples of gold in settings of silver.

—Proverbs 25:11

WORD EXORCISES

Deleting weak words week by week

Adopt the modest goal of deleting two weak words per week and you will rid yourself of one hundred unwanted words in less than a year's time.

What is the cost of a word?

According to *Business Week,* the orange growers paid the raisin growers $250,000 for the privilege of using the word **Sunkist.** If you ask me, the orange growers got a bargain, for the aura that surrounds the word **Sunkist** evokes such a positive response.

But negative words are costly, too. To date, cost analysts have not put a dollars-and-cents figure on negative words. But the cost is there all the same and it is enormous.

To my certain knowledge, the words *ain't* and *youse* have cost quite a few jobs. I also know of turndowns as a result of pronouncing **Illinois** incorrectly and of saying the word **Realtor*** as though it had *la* in the middle instead of **al.**

***Realtor:** A real-estate agent affiliated with the National Association of Real Estate Boards.

Please don't assume that a college degree—or even a graduate degree—assures you an error-free vocabulary. It doesn't. For too long we've emphasized adding words to the vocabulary. Careful and deliberate deletion of words is just as important. So is careful scrutiny and refinement of the words and phrases we intend to keep in our word storehouse. You'll notice I've included not only words for deletion but also words that require this careful scrutiny.

Some of the words in the exorcise section appear elsewhere in the book. This is deliberate. I did it for the purpose of reinforcement. Then, too, it's easy to skip certain sections of a book and miss the total message. I don't want this to happen to you.

There is no need to wait until the start of a new year to begin building a vital and vigorous vocabulary. Begin at the appropriate spot as soon as you acquire the book, and don't stop until you've completed all the material.

These exorcises will be doubly effective if you will also identify and include two words each week that are your special troublemakers.

JANUARY

One kind word can warm three winter months.

—JAPANESE PROVERB

January, the first month of the year, is named for the Roman god Janus (pronounced **jay-nus**).

Although Janus is usually shown with two faces—one looking forward and the other backward—he represents the beginning of things. This is because he was the god of doors and gates in Roman mythology. People used to pray to him when they were about to begin something new.

So pray if you wish, but do accompany your prayers with action; specifically, making this the year you rid yourself of verbal garbage.

January is the month of cruises. If you're lucky enough to go on one, don't embarrass yourself by calling an **ocean**

liner a *boat*. Since ships carry lifeboats, this should be an easy way to remember the correct word.

Thoughts of travel also serve as reminders to use the correct place name and to pronounce it correctly. Examples:

- It is **Algiers** (with an **s** at the end).
- It is **Tangier** (without an **s**).
- It is the **Sahara** and not the **Sahara Desert** (**Sahara** means "desert" in Arabic, so don't say *desert* twice).
- Say **Katahdins** rather than the **Katahdins mountains** (*Mountains* is inherent in **Katahdins,** of American Indian derivation, so you don't need to say *mountains* twice).

While you're at it, do remember that the **s** in **Illinois** is silent, and that **Spokane** is pronounced as though the second syllable were **can** and not *cane*.

No matter where you wander, if you wonder how the name of the place is pronounced, ask someone who knows. Usually the mayor of the town or a representative from the chamber of commerce can give you the acceptable pronunciation.

Exorcises

First week:	**undoubtably**	There is no such word. The word you want is **undoubtedly.** Let's hear the **ted.**
	worsh	The word is **wash.**
Second week:	**wrench**	This word is acceptable if you're referring to a tool. It is not acceptable to say *I'm going to* wrench *out some clothes.* The correct word here is **rinse.** Nor is it acceptable to say *heartwrenching experience.* The correct word is **heartrending.**
	youse	Rid yourself of this word.

Third week:	**you know**	This phrase was the biggest "nay" vote getter in the Feeble-phrase Finder.
	okay	When used as a conversation filler, the word **okay** is an irritant to the listener. It is particularly irritating if you use it as a question. Let's rid ourselves of it. Okay? Another equally offensive filler is **uhm**—exorcise it!
Fourth week:	**bullion**	Pronounced **bool'•yən.** Refers to gold or silver with regard to quantity rather than value. The word is sometimes used to refer to gold or silver bars, ingots or plates.
	bouillon	Pronounced **boo'•yon.** A clear broth.

FEBRUARY

A man cannot speak but he judges and reveals himself. With his will, or against his will, he draws his portrait to the eye of others by every word. Every opinion reacts on him who utters it.

—RALPH WALDO EMERSON

The word **February** comes from the Latin word *Februarius,* which in turn comes from the word meaning "to purify." Let us work in this month of February toward the purification of our use of words.

How about starting our word purification with the word **February**? It's pronounced **feb'•rōō•er•ē.** Yes, I know, Walter Cronkite has persisted in dropping the first **r.** He can get away with doing so; such a practice can be hurtful to the rest of us. While we're sounding **r**'s, it might be well to call attention to the word **library**. Let's sound both **r**'s in this word too.

Because Lent so often begins in February, this seems an appropriate time to include a couple of words that hurt the ears of ministers. The first is the word **offertory** (just four syllables—there is no **a** in the middle), and the second is **Revelation** as in the book of Revelation (no **s** at the end of the word).

Exorcises

First week:	**theirselves**	The word is **themselves.**
	somewheres	The word is **somewhere.**
Second week:	**preventative**	**Preventive** is preferred.
	prespiration	The word is **perspiration;** the first syllable is **per** and not *pre.*
Third week:	**recognizance**	"A bond or obligation binding a person to some act such as a court appearance."
	reconnaissance	"The examination or survey of a region; The activity of reconnoitering."
Fourth week:	**reoccur**	**Recur** is preferred.
	irregardless	The correct word is **regardless.**

MARCH

The Moving Finger writes; and having writ,
Moves on: nor all thy Piety nor Wit
Shall lure it back to cancel half a Line,
Nor all thy Tears wash out a Word of it.
            —Edward Fitzgerald's translation of
               Omar Khayyam Edition 1 (the *Rubáiyát*)

March was the first month of the ancient Roman calendar and was called *Martius*. When Julius Ceasar revised the calendar, he moved the beginning of the year from March to January. The name **March** honors Mars, the Roman god of war.

Because March is named for the god of war, let's make war on all words and phrases that dampen the enthusiasm of others. There are killer phrases that don't produce "hear"-ache to the listening ear but that do produce an ache to the spirit of the listener. I'm thinking of phrases such as:

"You decide."

"I don't care."

"Forget it."

"No way."

"It doesn't matter."

"We've tried that before."

"I know just what you're going to say."

March is a good time to bury such conversational cripplers.

Exorcises

First week: **pitcher** "A container made of glass, china, silver, or other material, with a handle at one side and a lip at the other." Do not confuse with:

picture "A drawing, painting, portrait, or photograph." Be careful to have a **k** sound in the first syllable; it is pronounced **pik′•chər.**

Second week: **onct** The correct word is **once.** No **t** at the end.

twict The correct word is **twice.** No **t** at the end.

Third week: **humble** Sound the **h** at the beginning of this word.

	height	There is a t at the end of this word. It rhymes with kite. Learn to spell it and you won't want to put a **th** at the end.
Fourth week:	**violet**	This is the flower for March. Learn to use all three syllables in pronouncing the word.
	gene*a*logy	Pronounced **jē•nē•äl′•ə•jē.** I'll bet if you learn to spell it, you'll also pronounce it correctly. It refers to the record of the descent of a family; lineage.

APRIL

Words are both better and worse than thoughts; they express them, and add to them; they give them power for good or evil; they start them on an endless flight, for instruction and comfort and blessing, or for injury and sorrow and ruin.

—TRYON EDWARDS

April, the fourth month of the year, is named for *Aprilis. Aprilis* is a Latin word meaning "to open." Let's designate April as the month to open—to actually clear—any clogged lines of communication.

There are soft, comforting words and phrases that can ease tensions. Learn to use them and you'll improve all your relationships.

Here are a few examples of soothing words and phrases:

• **Second mother** sounds warmer and less formal than *stepmother.* In fact, I tested the word *stepmother* in word clinics. When I asked what word, what adjective, fits the word *stepmother,* most respondents said "cruel." **Mother,** or even **second mother,** does not evoke a negative response. Adoptive mothers and fathers can be spared much pain if their children refer to their natural or birth parents in that way rather than making a distinction between "real" parents and adoptive ones. The happiest adoptive relationship I know is enhanced because the children refer to their adoptive mother as **mother** and to their late mother—whom they remember well—as their **first mother.**

• Words have a bearing on the in-law relationship too. It sounds friendlier to say, **I'd like you to meet Mary's mother,** than it does to say, *This is my mother-in-law.*

• And **I'll always remember** is more effective than *I'll never forget.*

Exorcises

First week:	**diamond**	April's birthstone is the **diamond.** Please make it three syllables.
	palm	Palm Sunday often arrives in April. When it does, do pronounce **palm** correctly (the l is sounded).
Second week:	**it don't**	**It doesn't** is correct. *It don't* is a contraction of *it do not.*
	between you and I	It is **between you and me.**
Fourth week:	**consensus of opinion**	**consensus**
	each and every	Use one or the other—not both.

MAY

Not in books only, nor yet in oral discourse, but often also in words there are boundless stores of moral and historic truth, and no less of passion and imagination laid up, from which lessons of infinite worth may be derived.

—RICHARD WHATELY

Believe what you choose about how May was named. Some educators say that **May** is short for *majores,* the Latin word for older men. These same educators say that June was considered sacred to the *juniores* or young men. I lean toward the popular view that May was named for Maia, the Roman goddess of spring and growth.

The most famous horse race in the United States, the Kentucky Derby, takes place on the first Saturday in May at Churchill Downs, Louisville, Kentucky. May, then, is a good time to polish our use of a couple of words that relate to horses. The word **equine** ("pertaining to or characteristic of a horse") rhymes with **mine, ē•kwīn.** And do take a good look at the word **jodhpurs.** *You'll notice that it's* **hp** *there in the middle of the word and not* **ph,** *so pronounce it accordingly. Yes, say* **jod•poors.**

May is also the month in which we observe Memorial Day. It's appropriate to mention that to call it *Decoration Day* is not considered quite so "upscale" or "on-top-of-it" as to call it **Memorial Day.**

Because many students become graduates or former students in May, let's also pause to study the word **alumnus.**

Exorcises

First week:	**alumnus**	This is the masculine singular form. Say **uh•lum′•nus.**
	alumni	This is the masculine plural form. It is also used to refer to a group of *men and women.* Say **uh•lum′•nī.**
	alumna	This is the feminine singular form. Say **uh•lum′•nuh.**
	alumnae	This is the feminine plural. Say **uh•lum′•nee.**
Second week:	**can**	**Can** refers to capability. For example: **I can finish this typing today.**
	may	Refers to permission or possibility. For example: **May I**

		borrow your pen? I may need it.
Third week:	**incidently**	The word is **incidentally.** Do notice that it has five syllables.
	bovine	If you'll remember that part of the word is **vine,** you'll probably pronounce it correctly. It is **bō•vīn** ("of or pertaining to a cow or a member of the cow family").
Fourth week:	**we was**	Say **we were.**
	we done	Say **we did.**

JUNE

No man has a prosperity so high or firm, but that two or three words can dishearten it; and there is no calamity which right words will not begin to redress.
> —RALPH WALDO EMERSON

Many authorities believe the Romans named June for Juno, the patron goddess of marriage. Others believe the name was taken from *juniores,* the Latin word for young men.

Since June is the month of weddings, it's fitting to give some thought to the words we use at this time. If ever "out-of-it" and "on-top-of-it" words take on importance, it's when we marry. My first awareness of this came about years ago through a discussion with a society editor. This is what she actually told me, "I can tell a lot about a family's background by the words they use in the write-up of the engagement or wedding. If they refer to a 'honeymoon' instead of a 'wedding trip,' or if they say, 'bride and groom' instead of 'bride and bridegroom,' I know that it [the wedding] is not a distinguished affair." When I asked if this influenced the amount of newspaper space allotted to the event, I received only a wry smile in answer.

Before you blast the society editor—or me—I should report that many cultured people agree with her assessment. Further, I should also report that many newspapers insist on the use of "wedding trip" and "bride and bridegroom" in describing nuptials.

I see that I have another *flag* in my notes for the month of June. It's this reminder: The Wimbledon Championships (premier event of tennis) have passed the one hundredth anniversary, yet many sportscasters persist in pronouncing the name **Wimbledon** incorrectly. I guess the trick is to first learn to spell the word. Do notice that there is a **b** in the middle instead of a **p** and that the final syllable is **don** and not **ton.**

Exorcises

First week:	fiancé	The word has three syllables. It's **fē•än•sā′.** "A man engaged to be married."
	fiancée	This word has the same pronunciation as the masculine word **fiancé.** "A woman engaged to be married."
Second week:	congratulations	Do note that the word has a **t** in the middle and not a **d.** It is proper to congratulate the bridegroom, but it is not proper to congratulate the bride; you may congratulate the happy couple.
	best wishes	Good wishes may be offered to either the bride or the bridegroom.
Third week:	The Reverend Mister (or Doctor) Brown	It is not considered good form to refer to the minister as *Reverend So-and-So;* put a **the** in front of it if you're referring to him or her. If

addressing him or her, use the desired designation, **Mr., Dr., Ms., Miss,** or **Mrs.**

champagne The purists insist that **champagne** comes only from Champagne (a region and former province of northeastern France). I mention it just so you'll know. The rest of us use the word to refer to sparkling white wine.

Fourth week: **candelabrum** "A large decorative candlestick." This is the singular form of the word. If you'll notice that the first part of the word is spelled **can•de** (instead of *candle*) you'll say it right.

candelabra This is the plural form of the word. It means "a large candlestick having several arms or branches."

medium This is the singular form of the word. For example, **Radio is a popular medium.**

media This is the plural form of the word. For example, **The news media were here.**

JULY

The knowledge of words is the gate of scholarship.
—JOHN WILSON

July was the fifth month in the calendar of the ancient Romans. It was called *Quintilis,* meaning "fifth." When Julius

Caesar, who was born in July, rearranged the calendar, he named the month for himself.

July seems to be the month of independence worldwide. Canada celebrates July 1 as Dominion Day. The United States celebrates July 4 as Independence Day; it is also celebrated as Independence Day in the Philippines. The celebration of independence takes place on July 5 in Venezuela; on July 9 in Argentina; on July 21 in Belgium; on July 25 in the Netherlands; and on July 28 in Peru. France celebrates Bastille Day on July 14.

July is a good time to think of words that relate to our independence. There is **government,** for example. Let's remember to sound the **n** in the middle of the word. And let's remind ourselves that the full title of the chief justice is **chief justice of the United States** (not *chief justice of the Supreme Court*).

If you happen to visit Washington, D.C., as so many do in July, do include a visit to the Smithsonian Institution. Please call it the Smithsonian **Institution** and not the Smithsonian *Institute.*

Exorcises

First week:	**cold slaw**	It is **cole slaw;** not *cold slaw.*
	sherbert	It is **sherbet.** The second syllable is **bet,** not *bert.*
Second week:	**bretzel**	There is no such word; it is **pretzel.**
	marshmellow	They may be mellow but the second part of the word is **mallow.** It is **marshmallow.**
Third week:	**ek cetera**	It is not *ek cetera* but **et cetera.** Please sound the **t** in the word **et.**
	exp*ear*ament	The word is **experiment;** there is no *spear* sound in the word.
Fourth week:	**excape**	There is no such word as

> *excape;* the word is **escape.**
> Sound that **s** in the first syl-
> lable.
>
> **enthused**   **Enthusiastic** is the correct
> word.

AUGUST

*Learn the value of a man's words and expressions, and you
know him. Each man has a measure of his own for everything; this he offers you inadvertently in his words. He who
has a superlative for everything wants a measure for the
great or small.*

— JOHN CASPAR LAVATER

August was the sixth month of the year in the early Roman
calendar. They called it *Sextilis,* meaning "sixth." When
the Emperor Augustus renamed the month for himself, he
also lengthened it to thirty-one days. In case you're won-
dering, he took the extra day from February.

August is a good time to take a look at words such as
drought and **temperature** and **vegetables.** You'll notice that
drought ends with a **t** and is therefore pronounced **drout.**
The word **drouth** has also gained acceptance. Both refer to
a long dry period. The word **temperature** is often used
when we mean **fever.** A few years ago one of my favorite
talk show hosts (nationally syndicated) mentioned that
"Reggie Jackson has a temperature and therefore can't play
baseball today." Three people told me about it. Who
knows how many called the station. Of course, Reggie has
a temperature. Don't we all? And this reminds me of the
doctor who was asked by an anxious wife if her husband,
the patient, had blood pressure. "Yes," the doctor replied,
"and it's a little low."

The preferred pronunciation of **vegetable** is **vej´•tə•bəl,**
although **vej´•ət•ə•bəl,** is also correct. But, please, don't use
the word *veggies!*

Exorcises

First week: **anxious**   "Uneasy because of thoughts or fears about what could happen; troubled."

                  eager   "Wanting very much."

Second week: **larnyx**   There is no such word; the word you want is **larynx.** It is pronounced **lar′•ingks.**

            temperature   Be sure to pronounce all four syllables.

Third week: **adverse**   "Hostile; antagonistic in design or effect." **Adverse** circumstances.

               averse   "Unwilling." Careful speakers and writers make a distinction between the words **averse** and **adverse.** To be **averse** to something expresses opposition on the subject's part. That which is **adverse** to a person or thing denotes opposition contrary to the person's will.

Fourth week: **regard**   "Consider, consideration; care for, respect; look at."

              regards   "Good wishes"; he sends his **regards.** One would say **in** or **with regard to** but not *in* or *with regards to.*

SEPTEMBER

Words may be either servants or masters. If the former they may safely guide us in the way of truth. If the latter they intoxicate the brain and lead into swamps of thought where there is no solid footing.

Among the sources of those innumerable calamities which

*from age to age have overwhelmed mankind, may be reck-
oned as one of the principal, the abuse of words.*
                                            —BISHOP GEORGE HORNE

September retains the name that comes from the Latin
septem, meaning "seven." In the old Roman calendar it
was the seventh month; hence the name **September** was appropriate. It became the ninth month when Julius Caesar
changed the calendar.

Because Labor Day is celebrated on the first Monday of
the month in Canada and the United States, it's an excellent time to review words that relate to work.

Certainly if you want to become a **Realtor,** you should
know that the first part of the word is **real,** not *re•la,* and
that it is usually capitalized. If you study to become an **ophthalmologist**—or if you visit one—learn that there is a **ph** in
the first syllable of the word and that it gets the **f** sound.
And take a good look at the word **veterinarian.** Granted
it's a mouthful, but do sound all six syllables.

Even though President Eisenhower mispronounced the
word **nuclear,** that doesn't excuse the rest of us. The word
is **noo′•kle•ər:** not *noo•kyoo•lər.*

Exorcises

First week:	**manufacture**	The second syllable is **u,** not **uh.**
	periodontist	Dentists who specialize in periodontics complain that many persons omit the first **o** both in pronunciation and in spelling.
Second week:	**criterion**	This is the single form of the word; do not interchange with **criteria,** the plural form of the word.
	phenomenon	This is the singular form of the word.
	phenomena	This is the plural form.

Third week:	**prostate**	Refers to a gland.
	prostrate	Lying face down in submission or adoration or from the heat.
Fourth week:	**creek**	"A small stream of water; a brook." Do not confuse with **crick.**
	crick	The word rhymes with **sick.** It refers to a muscle spasm.

I can't resist telling you why I take delight in including **phenomenon** and **phenomena.** In promoting the first edition of *Word Watcher's Handbook,* I was a guest of Fred Griffith on Cleveland's "The Morning Exchange." I was thrown completely off-balance when an off-camera assistant scribbled a note during our interview. The note said, "Talk about the word phenomen*um.*" For a couple of minutes there I thought the assistant knew something I didn't. Luckily, Mr. Griffith is truly professional. Very smoothly, he began a discussion of the words **phenomen*on*** and **phenomen*a*.** Then, when he perceived that my panic had subsided, he turned to me for a discussion of the words **criteria** and **criterion.**

OCTOBER

The weaker the ideas, the stronger the language. A person whose thinking lacks substance often laces it with profanity in an effort to give it muscle. In a word—he's intellectually bankrupt.

—ANN LANDERS

Although October is the tenth month of the year, its name derives from its having been the eighth month in the Roman calendar. Attempts to change the name didn't work; the Roman Senate tried to name the month *Antonius* after a Roman emperor, *Fautinus* after his wife, and *Tacitus* after a Roman emperor, but the people persisted in calling it **October.**

Let's celebrate the month of October by giving the **o** sound to words that require it: words such as **piano, potato, Ohio, window,** and **fellow.**

A television-station manager told me that if there hadn't been a piano near a window when he applied for his first job as an announcer, he might have been hired. You guessed it, he referred to the pian*uh* near the wind*uh*. Fortunately, he asked his interviewer why he was turned down, and, as he put it, "I haven't committed those sins since."

October is also a good time to remember that **Halloween** is a hallowed time, not a h*o*llow one. And that **pumpkin** is pronounced **pump'•kin.** If you'll pick plump pumpkins, you'll remember that **plump** and **pump** rhyme and have no more trouble.

Exorcises

First week:	**Eyetalian**	There is no such word; it is **Italian.** Think of the word **Italy** and it won't trouble you; you wouldn't say *Eyetaly.*
	ain't	Yes, I know that some dictionaries include this word, but it still hurts many ears.
Second week:	**accidently**	The word is **accidentally** and it has five syllables.
	most unique	**Unique** means "one of a kind." You don't need to qualify the word.
Third week:	**less**	**Less** means "not so much." Say **fewer** when you refer to something that can be counted. Beer that has **fewer** calories is **less** filling.
Fourth week:	**amount**	**Amount** means "aggregate." We use **amount** when we

think of things in terms of bulk. **Number** refers to things you can count. The **number** of assignments was higher in his class. The **amount** of time wasted was very small.

NOVEMBER

Words are but the signs and counters of knowledge, and their currency should be strictly regulated by the capital which they represent.

—CALEB C. COLTON

In the Roman calendar, November was the ninth month; it was named for *novem,* the Latin word for nine. Tiberius Caesar refused the Roman Senate's offer to name November for him after November became the eleventh month. As he refused, he asked, "What will you do if you have thirteen emperors?" So July (for Julius Caesar) and August (for Augustus Caesar) remain the only two months named for Roman emperors.

At the top of my notes for November I have this reminder: A **turkey** is a bird; do not refer to your friends as turkeys. Also, I see this: Honor the veterans on **Veteran's Day** by pronouncing **veteran** correctly. The word has three syllables.

I don't need a reminder to think of food in connection with November. My taste buds are aquiver at memories of Thanksgivings past and words such as **succulent** and **savory** abound. But back to the business at hand. This is a good time to remember that the **h** in **thyme** is silent, that **pâté** has two syllables, that **vichyssoise** is pronounced **vish'•ē•swaź** and that **rarebit** is not rabbit. And if you can't say **Chablis** as **sha•blē,** it's best to order white wine with your turkey.

Exorcises

First week:	**culinary**	If you'll think of the word cute, you'll say this correctly. It's **kyoo′•lə•nə′r•ē**.
	cuisine	Pronounce it **kwi•zē′n**.
Second week:	**herb**	The **h** is silent.
	human	Sound the **h**.
Third week:	**quiche**	Say **kēsh**.
	kebab	Even though the second syllable is spelled **bab**, it is pronounced **bob**.
Fourth week:	**hors d'oeuvre**	Say **ôr•durv′**. The pronunciation is the same for the plural form, **hors d'oeuvres**.
	gourmet	My friend Emilie Jacobson included this comment in a recent letter: "I still remember Ogden Nash, a *great* purist, sitting in my office growling, '**Gourmet** is not an adjective.'" Let's remember that the word is a noun and that it's pronounced **goŏr•mā′**.

DECEMBER

There are words which sever hearts more than sharp swords; there are words the point of which sting the heart through the course of a whole life.

—Frederika Bremer

December, the twelfth and last month of our calendar year, was so named because it was originally the tenth month of the year in the ancient Roman calendar. *Decem* means "ten" in Latin.

If you live in Zinzinnati—whoops, I mean Cincinnati—

you'll understand my warning about putting a z in the word **December.** Those of us with German or Dutch backgrounds tend to introduce a z sound every chance we get. The z sound in the second syllable of **December** must irritate a great many ears, for I've received a number of notes about it. The z sound in the word **sink** has also incurred a few complaints. One person took the trouble to explain, "In the old days sinks were made of zinc, maybe that's why people still say *zink* when they mean **sink.** Anyway, put a stop to it, will you?" I'll try.

Another of my December reminders has a sketch of Santa Claus pointing to the North Pole. Underneath the sketch I've written, "talk about **arctic.**" I believe that is to remind me to remind you that the word **arctic** has two c's and both are sounded.

There is also a note about **Hanukkah,** the Jewish Feast of Lights, or Feast of Dedication. The word is usually pronounced **Hah′•noo•kah** (spellings vary; it is Hanukkah, Hanukah, or Chanukah).

And there is this reminder: Many Christians are pained by the use of the word *Xmas* for **Christmas.** I'll pass along this comment: "The fact that **x** is often used to represent the unknown factor or quantity is no comfort."

Exorcises

First week:

poinsettia It is pronounced **poin-•sĕt•ē′ə.** The flower/shrub is named for J. R. Poinsett, a minister to Mexico.

fiscal "Of or pertaining to finances." Do note that the word has just two syllables.

Second week:

Calvary Place near Jerusalem where Christ was crucified. I always remember the distinction between **Calvary** and **cavalry** by associating **Calvin** (the great Christian) with **Calvary** and the word **cavalier** (which comes from the word **horseman**) with **cavalry**. The sequence of letters does it for me.

	cavalry	Has to do with horses. See above.
Third week:	**can't hardly**	*Can't hardly* is a double negative and should be avoided. Say **can hardly.**
	giblet	It is pronounced **jib'•let.**
Fourth week:	**grievous**	Say **grē'•vus.** Causing grief.
	suspicion	You have a **suspicion;** you **suspect.** Do not say, *"I suspicion."*
Bonus word:	**decimate**	This is from the Latin *decem* (ten). It means, literally, to "select by lot and kill one in every tcn." Many persons (nonpurists) use it to mean "kill or destroy a large number."

10

COMING TO TERMS: A WORD WATCHER'S GLOSSARY

I went to a lot of trouble to include this glossary of abbreviations and terms because I hope to spare you the embarrassment of feeling out of it—as I've felt on a number of occasions—when I didn't understand the conversation going on about me.

Please don't bandy these terms about in order to show how informed you are. You'll risk making some other soul feel out of it.

True communicating means *exchanging* thoughts or messages with someone else; to do that effectively both sender and receiver must understand the words used in the exchange.

GENERAL BUSINESS TERMS

abstract: a summary of important points

ACD: automatic call distributor—part of the telephone or other equipment that automatically dials into a terminal or to another telephone

ad hoc: with respect to a particular thing, for a specific purpose, case, or situation; often an ad hoc committee is formed to carry out a specific item on an agenda

ADP: automatic data processing

ad val/ad valorem: according to value (Latin)

AP: Associated Press

ASAP: as soon as possible

BBA: bachelor of business administration

BBB: Better Business Bureau

B/L: bill of lading

BSc: bachelor of science

BTU: British thermal unit

CCTV: closed circuit television

CD: certificate of deposit; compact disc

CEO: chief executive officer

CFA: chief financial analyst

CFO: chief financial officer

CIF: central information file; also, cost, insurance, and freight—the sender is responsible for the goods until they arrive safely at their final destination

COD: cash on delivery

COLA: cost of living adjustment

consignment: goods given to another for sale

consortium: a group of persons that pools its resources (financial or otherwise)

CORE: Congress of Racial Equality

COS: cash on shipment; also, chief of staff

CPA: certified public accountant

CPI: consumer price index—a monthly measure, put out by the federal government, of selected goods and services consumed by individuals

CRT: cathode-ray tube

DBA: doing business as

debenture: a bond backed solely by the credit standing of the issuer—no assets are pledged as security

demurrage: detention of a ship, freight car, or other cargo conveyance during loading or unloading beyond the scheduled time of departure, or the compensation paid for this detention

DOT: Department of Transportation; also, *Dictionary of Occupational Titles*

EDP: electronic data processing

EEOC: Equal Employment Opportunity Commission

E-mail: electronic mail

entrepreneur: someone who starts and manages a business enterprise; lately, this word has taken on a broader meaning—it can refer to someone who is in charge of a specific part of the business within a large organization

EOM: end of month

equity: the value of a property or business after any liability against it has been deducted; also, investments that signify ownership (stocks) as opposed to indebtedness (bonds) are referred to as equities

ERISA: Employee Retirement Income Security Act

est: Erhard Seminars Training, a philosophical movement started by Werner Erhard

ETA: estimated time of arrival

exempt employee/nonexempt employee: refers to whether or not an employee is subject to the provisions of the wage-and-hour law

fast track: what you are on if you are advancing professionally at a rapid clip

FCC: Federal Communications Commission

FDA: Food and Drug Administration

FICA: Federal Insurance Contributions Act

FIFO: first in, first out

FITW: Federal Income Tax Withholding

flextime: an arrangement whereby the employer and employee agree on flexible working hours

FM: frequency modulation

FOB: free on board—the sender is responsible for the goods until they are safely on board the truck, plane, train, or ship

franchise: an agreement between a manufacturer and a distributor or dealer to sell the manufacturer's goods or products on an exclusive basis within the territory

FRS: Federal Reserve System

FTC: Federal Trade Commission

FX: foreign exchange

FY: fiscal year

FYI: for your information

GAAP: generally accepted accounting procedures

garnishment: a legal attachment to an employee's wages to pay a debt owed to someone other than the employer

glitch: snag, snarl, error

Glyme's Formula for Success: the secret of success is sincerity; once you can fake that, you've got it made

GNP: gross national product

golden handshake/golden parachute: terms used to refer to the separation settlement or early retirement package offered to a long-term employee

Gresham's Law: bad money pushes good money out of circulation

Gresham's Law of Projects: trivial projects tend to displace the more demanding but more worthwhile projects

Gumperson's Law: if nothing can possibly go wrong, something will

hands-on: usually used as "hands-on experience"; it means the actual experience of doing the work

headhunter: slang expression for executive-search consultant—someone who finds appropriate executives for specific job openings within a client corporation

human resources: this is the field of work we used to refer to as "personnel"; it encompasses much more than the hiring and firing of personnel

IRA: individual retirement account

IRS: Internal Revenue Service

ITC: International Trade Commission

jobber: a person who buys from a producer and sells to a retailer

journeyman: a fully qualified crafts worker, generally one who has mastered the trade by serving an apprenticeship

Keogh: a tax-deferred investment for a self-employed person

LCL: less-than-carload lot

LIFO: last in, first out

"line" manager: usually has direct responsibility for results (*see* "staff" manager)

L*S*I*T*T: let's stick it to them

M & A's: mergers and acquisitions

manifest: an itemized list of cargo

MBA: master of business administration

MBO: management by objectives

microfiche: a sheet of microfilm that contains rows of microimages of pages of printed matter

microfilm: a film upon which documents are photographed and greatly reduced in size

MIS: management information systems; yes, managing these systems is called MIS management

monitor: a display device that can receive video signals by direct connection only

Murphy's Law: if anything can go wrong, it will

NLRB: National Labor Relations Board

OAG: *Official Airline Guide*

OSHA: Occupational Safety and Health Act

outplacement: placement help for the person on the way "out"

Pareto's Law: twenty percent of anything takes eighty percent of application

Parkinson's Corollary: expenditures rise to meet and slightly exceed income

Parkinson's Law: the task expands to meet the time available for its completion

PBX: private branch exchange

perk: perquisite—a reward or privilege provided in addition to your regular salary; membership in a country club is an example

The Peter Principle: people in organizations tend to rise to their level of incompetence

phone mail: messages stored on a telephone answering machine or system

P & L: profit and loss

pro rata: in proportion

prospectus: a formal summary of a proposed venture

quality circles: a Japanese management innovation that involves non-management people in operational decisions; essentially the same principle as participative management with work teams

QC: quality control

QED: *quod erat demonstrandum*—which was to be demonstrated (Latin)

quid pro quo: an equal exchange or substitution—something for something

R & D: research and development

SBA: Small Business Administration

SCORE: Service Corps of Retired Executives

SEC: Securities and Exchange Commission

SIG: special interest group

"skunk works": referred to in *In Search of Excellence* (*see* Bibliography) as a small band of mavericks monomaniacally working to get a particular task done; Li'l Abner fans may remember the skunk works that Earthquake McGoon worked in

SOP: standard operating procedure

"staff" manager: usually is responsible for support to the "line" function

survivorship: the right of a surviving partner or joint owner to the entire assets that were originally jointly owned

TA: transactional analysis

TVA: Tennessee Valley Authority

TWX: teletypewriter exchange

UPC: Universal Product Code

UPI: United Press International

VCR: videocassette recorder

VIP: very important person

VTR: videotape recorder

WATS lines: Wide Area Telecommunications Service lines

wpm: words per minute

COMPUTER TERMS

And now, we get technical.

If you're a technophobe—like me—you'll need all the help you can get to understand the ubiquitous computer. So, take this part bit by bit and you won't risk over-"byte."

If you're *into* computers, please don't quarrel with my definitions unless you can simplify them still further.

architecture: a set of specifications for a computer system

BASIC: Beginner's All-purpose Symbolic Instruction Code, a programming language developed by Dartmouth College; especially well suited to personal computers and beginning users.

binary code: a number system that use only two digits, 0 and 1; a number or letter can be expressed as a combination of these digits; computers translate each character of information into a string of binary numbers

bit: the smallest unit or bit of information; short for binary digit

byte: a single unit of information, or one space in the computer memory—for personal computers a byte is usually eight bits

CAD/CAM: computer-aided design/computer-aided manufacturing

chip: a waferlike disk of silicon and metal etched with miniature circuitry

COBOL: Common Business-Oriented Language; a programming language that is well suited to business applications involving complex data records and large amounts of printed output

CPU: central processing unit—brains of the system

CRT: cathode-ray tube, like a television screen

curser: humanoid who is trying to learn to operate the computer

cursor: little blinking square, line, or other marker to show you where on the screen the work is being done

data: letters, numbers, facts, and symbols for use by the computer

disk: rigid, flat, circular plate with a magnetic coating for storing data

diskette/floppy disk: flexible, flat, circular plate permanently housed in a paper envelope, with a magnetic coating that stores data; standard sizes are 3½, 5¼, or 8 inches in diameter

dot-matrix printer: prints letters and numbers with little dots

encode: to put a message into code

enterprise: a company or a division within a company

FORTRAN: stands for Formula Translation, a widely used high-level programming language; it is well suited to problems that can be expressed in algebraic formulas—generally used in scientific applications

graphics: refers to diagrams, mathematical drawings, or charts

hacker: someone who plays with computers, particularly someone who attempts the electronic invasion of data bases

hardware: the equipment that makes up a computer system: the keyboard, system box, and monitor (screen) are all hardware components

interface: connecting device; place where two or more independent systems meet and interact with each other, such as the interface between a computer and printer

magnetic media: any of several formats that can record and play back magnetic impulses

mainframe: a computer that is physically large and provides the capability to perform applications requiring large amounts of data, usually accessible from a number of terminals

microcomputer: a computer that is physically very small; personal and home computers are usually microcomputers

minicomputer: a type of computer whose physical size is usually smaller than a mainframe—for small-business use

mission critical: important

modem: comes from the term modulator/demodulator; a device that converts computer signals (or data) into high-frequency communications signals and vice versa; the signals can then be sent over telephone lines

networked: computers that are connected are said to be **networked**

on-line: having direct access to the computer; for example, airline reservation systems are **on-line**

PASCAL: a programming language that can be used on many microcomputers; it is considered more difficult to learn than BASIC, but it can generate programs that run faster and use less memory; the name comes from that of the French mathematician and philosopher Blaise Pascal

printer: the device that produces a paper copy of a document

RAM: random-access memory, the type of memory used in most computers to store the data and the instructions of programs currently being run

ROM: read-only memory, memory containing fixed data or instructions that are permanently loaded during the manufacturing process; a computer uses the data in ROM but cannot change it

software: computer programs (business systems, games, etc.) as distinguished from hardware (the computer itself); the instructions that tell a computer what to do

solution: a computer industry product; for example, a new software program

subroutine: in music we have a refrain (a theme that is repeated throughout the work); in computer talk the refrain is called a **subroutine**

terminal: keyboard plus either a CRT or a printer; a **smart terminal** also has some data-processing capability

text: words

video screen: monitor

VDT: video-display terminal

VT: video terminal

word processor: an electronic text-editing system that lets you compose and work with material on a video-display screen before printing it

word wrapping: the automatic shifting of words from a line that is too long to the next line

SATELLITE TERMS

dish: a bowl-shaped antenna to link an earth station with a satellite

downlink: a dish that receives signals from a satellite; the dish must be "tuned" to the satellite, as you would tune a television set to a channel

footprint: the geographic area that can receive satellite signals; it takes three satellites, strategically placed, to **footprint** the world

geostationary orbit: satellites are "parked" 22,300 miles above the earth, moving at the same speed as the earth rotates, so that they appear to stand still

narrowcasting: the opposite of *broad*casting; refers to a program that is geared to a narrow audience (learn this one—you're going to hear it often)

satellite: a communications vehicle put into orbit around the earth, and containing **transponders,** which receive, amplify, and retransmit signals

steerable: an uplink that can be "tuned"—as you would direct a flashlight beam—to hit any satellite

uplink: a dish that transmits signals to a satellite, to be bounced back to a downlink on earth; the transmit-receive process takes one quarter of a second

VF: video frequency; also, visual field

BIBLIOGRAPHY

The American Express Pocket Dictionary and Phrase Book English-Italian. New York: Simon and Schuster, 1983.

The American Heritage Dictionary. New York: New Dell Edition, Dell Publishing, 1984.

Bates, Jefferson D. *Writing with Precision*. Washington, D.C.: Acropolis Books Ltd., 1985.

Berlitz Italian for Travellers. Rev. ed. Lausanne, Switzerland: 1984.

Bernstein, Theodore M. *Bernstein's Reverse Dictionary*. Revised and expanded by David Grambs. New York: Times Books, 1988.

Bernstein, Theodore M. *The Careful Writer: A Modern Guide to English Usage*. New York: Atheneum, 1965.

Detz, Joan. *How to Write & Give a Speech*. New York: St. Martin's Press, 1984.

Flesch, Rudolph. *Say What You Mean*. New York: Harper & Row, 1972.

Fowler, H. W. *A Dictionary of Modern English Usage*. Revised by Sir Ernest Gowers. Oxford University Press, 1965.

Hamlin, Sonya. *How to Talk So People Listen*. New York: Harper & Row, 1988.

[Institute for Language Study] *Italian in a Nutshell*. New York: Funk & Wagnalls, 1967.

Kilpatrick, James J. *The Writer's Art*. Kansas City, Missouri: Andrews, McMeel & Parker, 1984.

Martin, Phyllis. *Martin's Magic Formula for Getting the Right Job*. Rev. ed. New York: St. Martin's Press, 1987.

Newman, Edwin. *A Civil Tongue*. New York: Warner Books, 1977.

Newman, Edwin. *I Must Say*. New York: Warner Books, 1988.

Newman, Edwin. *Strictly Speaking*. New York: Warner Books, 1974.

Roddick, Ellen. *Writing That Means Business*. New York: Macmillan, 1984.

Safire, William. *On Language*. New York: Times Books, 1980.

Safire, William. *Take My Word for It*. New York: Times Books, 1986.

Safire, William. *What's the Good Word?*. New York: Times Books, 1982.

Safire, William. *You Could Look It Up*. New York: Times Books, 1988.

Slutsky, Jeff. *Streetfighting*. Englewood Cliffs, N.J.: Prentice Hall, 1984.

Stewart, Marjabelle Young, and Faux, Marian. *Executive Etiquette*. New York: St. Martin's Press, 1979.

Strunk, William Jr., and White, E.B. *The Elements of Style*. 3rd ed. New York: Macmillan, 1979.

Walther, George R. *Phone Power*. New York: G. P. Putnam's Sons, 1986.

NOW A WORD FROM YOU, PLEASE

By permission of Johnny Hart and Creators Syndicate.

I welcome your comments about the third edition of *Word Watcher's Handbook*. While I don't wish to provoke the kind of outrage depicted in the cartoon; I do hope to provoke thought. I'm reporting on what hurts listeners' ears. I do not say that everything I've included here hurts my ears. Nor do I say I'm free of all the "hear"-ache I write about.

Those who replied to my last request (in the second edition of *Word Watcher's Handbook*) taught me that I have a lot to learn—and that you have a lot to teach me.

_ _

Phyllis Martin:

How about _____?

And shouldn't _____be _____?

Suggestion for your next edition _____

_____

Signed: (if you wish) _____

Student _____Education _____Age: under 21 _____

Occupation _____Sex _____   21 + _____

_ _

Order Form

Extra copies of *Word Watcher's Handbook* may be ordered directly from the publisher.

If you found this book useful, you might also be interested in *Martin's Magic Formula for Getting the Right Job,* a practical and result-oriented guide to job hunting. Both books may be ordered by writing to:

St. Martin's Press, 175 Fifth Avenue, New York, N.Y. 10010. Please make check or money order payable to St. Martin's Press.

Please send _____ copies of *Word Watcher's Handbook,* @ $6.95 each plus postage and handling charges of $2.00 for the first book and 75¢ for each additional book, to:

Name_____

Address_____

City_____ State_____ Zip_____

Please send _____ copies of *Martin's Magic Formula for Getting the Right Job,* @ $7.95 each plus postage and handling charges of $2.00 for the first book and 75¢ for each additional book, to:

Name _____

Address _____

City _____State _____Zip _____

INDEX

abbreviations, glossary of,
149–156
abjure/adjure, 53
"accidently" for "accidentally,"
144
adoption, words for family and,
134
adverse/averse, 54, 141
advice/advise, 54
affect/effect, 54
age, words as indicator of, 79
"ain't," 144
airline industry, abused and
misused words of, 120
Algiers, 129
allude/elude, 54
allusion/illusion, 54
Aloft, 80
alternately/alternative, 54
"alumna," 135
"almunae," 135
"alumni," 135
"alumnus," 135
American vs. British English,
105–111
"amount," 144–145
Anderson, Barbara, 91, 123
"anxious," 141
April, 133–134

"arctic," pronunciation of, 147
assure/ensure, 54
August, 140–141
authors, abused and misused
words of, 123–125
avenge/revenge, 54–55
"averse," 141
awareness test, 87–90
"ax" for "ask," 1

Baldrige, Malcolm, 6
banking industry, abused and
misused words of, 120
beside/besides, 55
"best wishes," 137
"between you and I" for "between
you and me," 134
biannual/biennial, 55
bouillon, pronunciation of, 130
"bovine," pronunciation of, 136
brand names, used generically,
86–87
Bremer, Frederika, 146
"bretzel" for "pretzel," 139
British vs. American English,
105–111
buddy system, pronunciation
mistakes spotted with, 62
"bullion," pronunciation of, 130

Business Week, 127
business
    abused and misused words of,
        120
    glossary of terms, 149–153
"busy as a bee," 21
"butcher" for "meat cutter," 121

Caesar, Augustus, 140, 145
Caesar, Julius, 138–139, 142, 145
Caesar, Tiberius, 145
Calvary/cavalry, 55, 147–148
"can," 135
"can't hardly," 148
"candelabra," 138
"candelabrum," pronunciation of,
    138
cement/concrete, 55
censor/censure, 55
ceramists, abused and misused
    words of, 121
"Chablis," pronunciation of, 145
"champagne," 138
charted/chartered, 55
"chief justice of the United
    States," 139
childish/childlike, 55
Cincinnati, 146–147
clarity of speech, 4
climactic/climatic, 55
"cold slaw" for "cole slaw," 139
collaborate/corroborate, 55–56
Colton, Caleb C., 145
communication, tips to improve
    your, 3–4
comprise/constitute, 56
computer terms, 154–156
"concensus of opinion," 134
"congratulations," 137
connive/contrive, 56
construction industry, abused and
    misused words of, 121
contemptible/contemptuous, 56
continual/continuous, 56
cost of words, 127–128

credible/credulous, 56
"creek," 143
"crick," 143
"criteria," 142–143
"criterion," 142–143
Cronkite, Walter, 130
"cuisine," pronunciation of, 146
"culinary," pronunciation of, 146

December, 146–148
"decimate," 148
deletionary, 11–35
    feeble-phrase finder, 21–34
    runners-up in, 20
deprecate/depreciate, 56
"diamond," pronunciation of, 134
dictionary
    pronunciation checked in, 62–63
    using a, 4
discreet/discrete, 56
disinterested/uninterested, 57
distrait/distraught, 57
downscale words, 79–80
"drought," 140
"drouth," 140

"each and every," 134
"eager," 141
editors, things that annoy,
    123–126
educational level, language as
    indicator of, 79
educators, abused and misused
    words of, 121
Edwards, Tryon, 133
Eisenhower, Dwight D., 142
"ek cetera" for "et cetera," 139
elicit/illicit, 57
Eliot, T. S., 79
Emerson, Ralph Waldo, 130, 136
emigrate/immigrate, 57
eminent/imminent, 57
English vs. American English,
    105–111
"enthused" for "enthusiastic," 140

"equine," pronunciation of, 135
"excape" for "escape," 139–140
Executive Etiquette (Young and Faux), 91
"exp*ear*ament" for "experiment," 139
"Eyetalian" for "Italian," 144

Fallon, Jim, 89
farther/further, 57
Faux, Marian, 91
faze/phase, 57
February, 130–131
feeble-phrase finder, 21–34
"fellow," pronunciation of, 144
"fever," 140
"fewer," 144
"fiancé," 137
"fiancée," 137
first mother, 134
"fiscal," 147
fiscal/physical, 57
Fitzgerald, Edward, 131
flair/flare, 57
flash cards
  pronunciation practice with, 63
  samples of, 6–9
  using, 3
flaunt/flout, 57
food industry, abused and misused words of, 121
foreign menu terms, 91–104
"forget it," 132
formally/formerly, 57
French menu terms, 92–100
  pronunciation key for, 100–101
funeral industry, abused and misused words of, 123

"genealogy," pronunciation of, 133
"giblet," pronunciation of, 148
"gourmet," 146
"government," 139

"grievous," 148
Griffith, Fred, 143

hair styling, abused and misused words of, 122
"Halloween," pronunciation of, 144
"Hanukkah," pronunciation of, 147
"have a nice day," 21
healthful/healthy, 58
"heartwrenching" for "heartrending," 129
"height," pronunciation of, 133
"herb," pronunciation of, 146
historic/historical, 58
Horne, Bishop George, 141–142
"hors d'oeuvre," pronunciation of, 146
horses, words related to, 135
"human," pronunciation of, 146
"humble," pronunciation of, 132

"I know just what you're going to say," 132
"I don't care," 132
Illinois, pronunciation of, 129
imply/infer, 58
important/importantly, 58
impracticable/impractical, 58
"incidently" for "incidentally," 136
Independence Day, 139
ingenious/ingenuous, 58
in-law relationship, words that have a bearing on, 134
"interface," 6
interior design, abused and misused words of, 122
"irregardless" for "regardless," 1, 131
"it don't" for "it doesn't," 134
"it doesn't matter," 132
Italian menu terms, 101–104

Jackson, Reggie, 140
January, 128–130
"jodhpurs," pronunciation of, 135
July, 138–140
June, 136–138

Katahdins, 129
"kebab," pronunciation of, 146
kind words, 6

Landers, Ann, 85, 90, 143
languishing/lavishing, 58
"larnyx," pronunciation of, 141
Lavater, John Caspar, 140
lectures, attending, 4
length of words, 3–4
"less," 144
Librairie Larousse, 91
"library," 131
lightning/lightening, 58
limp/limpid, 59
listening well, 5–6
loose/lose, 59
luxuriant/luxurious, 59

mantel/mantle, 59
"manufacture," pronunciation of,
    142
March, 131–133
marital/martial, 59
marriage, words related to,
    136–137
"marshmellow" for
    "marshmallow," 139
*Martin's Magic Formula for
    Getting the Right Job*
    (Martin), 80
May, 134–136
"may," 135–136
meantime/meanwhile, 59
media, 122, 138
medical profession, abused and
    misused words of, 121–122
"medium," 138

"Memorial Day," 135
menus, foreign words in, 91–104
minus words, 80, 85
misspellings, avoiding, 125–126
moral/morale, 59
"most unique," 144
"mother," response evoked by,
    133–134

nauseated/nauseous, 59
"needless to say," 6
negative listeners, 5–6
New York Times, The, 80
New Etiquette, The (Young), 91
"no way," 132
noisome/noisy, 59
November, 145–146
"nuclear," pronunciation of, 142
"number," 145

occupational hazards, 119–126,
    142
October, 143–145
"offertory," 123, 131
"Ohio," pronunciation of, 144
"okay," 130
Omar Khayyam, 131
"onct" for "once," 132
on-top-of-it words, 80–84
"ophthalmologist," pronunciation
    of, 142
out-of-it words, 80–84

"pâté," pronunciation of, 145
Packard, Vance, 79
"palm," pronunciation of, 134
partial/partly, 59
peak/peek, 59
"periodontist," 142
persecute/prosecute, 60
"phenomena," 142–143
"phenomenon," 142–143
"piano," pronunciation of, 144
"picture," pronunciation of, 132

pitch of your speech, 4
"pitcher," 1, 132
place names
    American vs. British, 110–111
    travel savvy and, 112–118
"plump," pronunciation of, 144
plus words, 80, 85
"poinsettia," 147
pore/pour, 60
positive listeners, 5
"potato," pronunciation of, 144
"prespiration" for "perspiration,"
    131
"preventative" for "preventive,"
    131
"prioritize," 6
pronunciation, 62–78
    mistakes in, 1–2
    using a tape to practice, 3
pronunciation key, 63
    French menu terms, 100–101
prostate/prostrate, 60, 143
publishing industry, abused and
    misused words of, 123–125
"pumpkin," pronunciation of, 144
purposefully/purposely, 60

"quiche," pronunciation of, 146
quizzes
    awareness test, 87–90
    travel savvy, 112–118

ravage/ravish, 60
reading, improving your speech
    with, 4
real estate, abused and misused
    words of, 123, 127, 142
"recognizance," 131
"reconnaissance," 131
"regard," 141
"regards," 141
regime/regimen, 60
regretfully/regrettably, 60
relevant/revelant, 60

religion, abused and misused
    words of, 123, 131
rend/render, 60
"reoccur" for "recur," 131
Reporter Typographics, 124
"Revelation," 123, 131
"Reverend," 137–138

Safire, William, 80
Sahara, 129
satellite terms, 156
"savory," 145
science, abused and misused
    words of, 123
"second mother" for
    "stepmother," 133–134
sensual/sexual, 60
September, 141–143
"sherbert" for "sherbet," 139
"sink," pronunciation of, 147
Smithsonian Institution, the, 139
"somewheres" for "somewhere,"
    131
soothing words and phrases,
    133–134
speakers, abused and misused
    words about, 123
spelling, 110
    American vs. British, 110
    most threatening words,
        125–126
"Spokane," pronunciation of, 129
Status Seekers, The (Packard), 79
Stewart, Marjabelle Young, 91
straight/strait, 60
"succulent," 145
"suspicion," for "suspect," 148

tack/tact, 60–61
Tangier, 129
tapes
    pronunciation practice with, 3,
        62
    using to practice words, 3

team/teem, 61
technical words, 119–126, 142
  glossary of, 149–156
television, what to watch on, 4
"temperature," 140–141
tests
  awareness test, 87–90
  travel savvy, 112–118
"theirselves" for "themselves,"
  131
"thyme," pronunciation of, 145
tortuous/torturous, 61
trademarks, misuse of, 86–87
travel experience, language as
  indicator of, 79
travel savvy, test of, 112–118
turbid/turgid, 61
"turkey," 145
"twict" for "twice," 132

"undoubtably" for
  "undoubtedly," 129
unique, 144
upscale words, 79–80
usage, 36–61
  unmatched pairs, 53–61

"vegetables," 140
venal/venial, 61
"veteran," pronunciation of, 145
"veterinarian," pronunciation of,
  142
"viable," 6

"vichyssoise," pronunciation of,
  145
"violet," pronunciation of, 133
visual images, using, 4
voice, modulating your, 4
volume of your voice, 4

wangle/wrangle, 61
"we done," for "we did," 136
"we was" for "we were," 136
"we've tried that before," 132
wedding, words related to,
  136–137
Whately, Richard, 134
Wilson, John, 138
Wimbledon, 137
"window," pronunciation of, 144
Word Watchers' Clinic, 21, 62
word exorcises, 127–128
word processor, using as
  deletionary, 6
work, words related to, 119–126,
  142
"worsh" for "wash," 129
"wrench," 129
Writer's Digest, 80

"Xmas" for "Christmas," 147

"you decide," 132
"you know," 21, 130
"youse," 129